HOW TO PASS

PROFESSIONAL LEVEL PSYCHOMETRIC TESTS

HOW TO PASS

PROFESSIONAL LEVEL PSYCHOMETRIC TESTS

2ND EDITION

Sam Al-Jajjoka

KOGAN PAGE

Whilst the author has made every effort to ensure that the content of this book is accurate, please note that occasional errors can occur in books of this kind. If you suspect that an error has been made in any of the tests included in this book, please inform the publisher at the address printed below so that it can be corrected at the next reprint.

Publisher's Note

Every possible effort has been made to ensure that the information contained in this book is accurate at the time of going to press, and the publishers and authors cannot accept responsibility for any errors or omissions, however caused. No responsibility for loss or damage occasioned to any person acting, or refraining from action, as a result of the material in this publication can be accepted by the editor, the publisher or the author.

First Indian Edition 2006

Kogan Page India Private Limited
4737/23, Ansari Road
Daryaganj
New Delhi 110 002.

ISBN 81-7554-301-9

Published by Vinod Vasishtha for Kogan Page India Private Limited, 4737/23, Ansari Road, Daryaganj, New Delhi 110 002. Printed and bound at Raj Press, R-3 Inderpuri, New Delhi - 110 0012.

I dedicate this book to my Dad, who died from a heart attack.
He was a terrific father and a remarkable human being.

Contents

Preface

As well as an increase in content, the second edition incorporates more psychometric tests and more examples to help candidates to practise and familiarize themselves with such tests before their assessment day. Before we begin, I would like to give you some of my own personal tips on passing and preparing for your assessment day.

Before you attend an assessment day, either visit your favourite library or career service or browse the Internet and do some research on the employer and industry that you are considering. Always keep in mind that employers want to see what you can do for them. After all, this is why the employer is inviting you for interview in the first place. The current job market may be the most competitive in recent history. There are simply too many applicants for too few well-paying, skilled positions and it is difficult for the employer to choose amongst thousands of candidates.

Make sure to proofread all your writing carefully before mailing. Have your CV and covering letter read by others. If you find yourself rushing to get something in the mail, take a moment to slow down and make sure you are sending out high-quality information – remember that the employer has to sift through thousands of applications, which is a very difficult job. A scruffy application creates a bad impression. Your career is in your hands.

The employer needs to feel that you took the time and effort to target their company specifically, that you take a special interest in working for them and that you have the abilities and personal qualities to do the job. This is why employers nowadays place such a strong emphasis on psychometric tests as measures of an applicant's skills. Psychometric tests identify your strengths and weaknesses in order to place you in the appropriate position. They measure whether you have specific abilities or appropriate personal qualities in relation to the job specification and whether you need further training to develop the necessary attributes. Such testing is usually much more effective than interview alone, according to most psychologists. The accepted view is that putting all the candidates through the same test is a fair way to make a final judgement, but alternatively lots of intelligent people may be excluded if their success is to depend on a 20–30-minute test. However, we are living in the real world and Human Resources departments want to produce statistics so that when you call for feedback on your interview they can tell you how you scored compared with other candidates. In this way you are satisfied as you have proof as to whether or not you performed to meet the organization's requirements. The employer is also happy because they can argue from a fair position in awarding the job.

If you are unfamiliar with psychometric tests you may be too nervous to do justice to your ability, or may waste valuable time just trying to understand what you are being asked to do. You will certainly be at a disadvantage compared with candidates who have already had practice with such tests. This is where this book comes in. It provides you with intelligent tips of the trade and hints that could help to get you a job offer.

I hope that this book enhances your understanding of a variety of psychometric tests and that familiarizing yourself with the different tests will give you courage and self-confidence to perform better. I guarantee that those who read this book will thank me if it helps them to do their best.

Acknowledgements

It was a hard job to find spare time and energy to write this book. However, I thank my software engineer colleagues in Germany, my students in the UK and various professionals for their perceptive comments and judgement.

Introduction

This book contains examples of the type of aggressive psychometric tests which may be encountered in IT, management and finance recruitment procedures, although some tests (Chapters 1, 2, 4 and 5) are relevant to other areas of employment too. The book is designed to work in tandem with other publications from Kogan Page, now used by thousands of students. The book assumes that you have been invited for interview or to an assessment centre, and are now preparing yourself for the big day.

However, even if you have never been invited for interview or to an assessment centre before, you will do just fine. This book is designed to be used as a stand-alone guide to test your abilities and the power of your brain to find out more about your own strengths and weaknesses. The book also makes the daring assumption that you are somebody special. There are too many books written for every possible candidate (the good, the bad and the ugly): this book is tailored for strong performers like you, applying for jobs in the IT, management and finance industries.

The selection process varies for most job requirements and the number of psychometric tests available in the market is enormous. The ones included in this book are based on my personal experience from talking to my students and attending interviews and assessment centres for small and large organizations. Also, in my previous job in Germany I found that similar psychometric tests are becoming part of employment requirements there. I am sure that when you start reading the book you will discover wonderful things about your ability that you did not know before and that could be used to impress the employer. The book provides step-by-step assistance and intelligent tips to help you perform better. Effective preparation using my methods of approaching problems, presented in this book, can greatly increase your chances of being selected, and can even result in getting a job. The book in your hands is about passing certain tests on your assessment day. I have taken the utmost care to provide exercises that are relevant and in common use currently. The book is designed to give you confidence in taking any kind of test in order to prepare and familiarize yourself with what is required. Although I cannot guarantee that all your tests will be exactly like the ones given here, I have tried to provide examples of the main kinds, so you can expect to meet something quite similar.

The book focuses only on the most popular tests used by the industry to select people best suited for professional positions, depending on the skills needed in the job. Other tests such as verbal aptitude tests, quantitative reasoning tests, personality questionnaires to see how you would react or behave in different situations, written exercises to demonstrate your written communication skills, and interviews to allow you to demonstrate oral communication skills are often included in big organizations' selection procedures. For this reason, I suggest you read other books and prepare yourself for likely questions during your interview. To reflect the time constraint you will face during actual tests, I have suggested a time for the completion of each test. The answers for each test can be found at the end of the relevant chapter, together with an explanation of the answers.

It is always a good idea, before an interview, to call the human resources department or ideally the person who contacted you and ask what sort of tests you will be required to undertake. Some organizations even send a simple flyer with some practice examples included in your invitation letter. This is only to give a flavour of what you should expect; it does not mean that only similar tests will be used. While it is sensible to concentrate on those tests, I have known of instances where an organization gave advance warning of only two tests, but surprised candidates on the day with another one never mentioned in their invitation letter or telephone call. Therefore, I recommend that you spend some time reading all the chapters and understanding all the exercises and tips, so that you will be less likely to get a shock on your assessment day.

The investment of time and effort to study the book and familiarize yourself with the types of questions that may be asked and tips for approaching them is an investment in your future. Take the time to read through most, if not all of the exercises in this book. There may be exercises that just apply to your assessment day.

Furthermore, while the exercises in this book are useful to start to teach you the basic skills, feel free, later, to deviate from them and build your own examples. Let your examples evolve. They will in all probability get better and better as your brain starts adjusting to a new challenge. It is like learning a new language. It is difficult to say a word or express your ideas at the beginning, then you become fluent and able to produce your own speech. Confidence and speed come with determination to do better, practice and familiarization.

What are psychometric tests?

Psychometric tests are multiple-choice questions (this does not necessarily apply to all the tests in this book) to be answered within a set time (and the timing is very tight) using pencil and paper, but they can be on a computer. They are designed to assess your reasoning abilities and whether you have specific skills in relation to the job specification or position for which you are being considered. The questions, in principle, need no further study or prior knowledge and are based on your logical reasoning or thinking performance. Of course, the more skills are being tested, the more psychometric tests you will be required to perform and the more accurate and comprehensive will be the picture of you built up by the employer. A typical test has a time limit allowing you between 25 and 60 minutes for 30 to 120 questions. Each question has only one correct answer, which is often to be selected from 3–5 alternatives (although tests exist that require more than one suggested answer to be identified as correct). Therefore, every incorrect alternative successfully identified and eliminated improves your chances of choosing the correct answer from the alternatives remaining. The questions are designed to become more difficult as you go through and are designed not to be completed within the given time unless you are a genius!

My advice is to read the instructions in each test, understand the practice examples at the beginning of the test to prepare for the real testing session and ask the assessor to clarify any ambiguity and then work through the questions as quickly and accurately as possible. Start with the ones you can answer accurately and if you are taking too long over a question, move on to the next one; if you have time you can go back later to finish the ones you did not manage to answer. Remember you don't get extra marks for finishing early and it is only the number of correct answers that counts. Sometimes negative marking is used, which means that you lose marks for incorrect answers. If this is the case, don't use guesswork to fill in your score sheet and try your best to answer correctly as many items as possible. However, if negative marking is not used, I advise the use of intelligent guessing to improve your score, by eliminating all the incorrect choices and making random guesses on the remaining ones.

Usually your results are compared with those of other candidates who have done the test in the past, which is called the norm group. In this way, the company will able to assess your reasoning skills in relation to others, and to make a judgement about your ability to cope with tasks involved in the job. If you take many psychometric tests during one assessment day, it is usually your overall performance that is important. However, this is not always the case, as I found out with one organization; when they sent the overall score sheet to one of my students his overall score was a pass but in two of the tests he scored less than the minimum required, and was in consequence not invited for the next stage.

Even if you don't feel confident about your performance in the psychometric tests, you may have other strengths, eg group exercise, writing skills, leadership, ad hoc experience etc, all of which will be taken into account and might compensate for your weakness. Finally, always, even if you fail, ask the employer for feedback about your performance. This may help you to pinpoint your weaknesses in order to work on them in the future and learn from the experience; it may also aid you in deciding your career path.

General remarks about your psychometric test day

- Discuss your test with your careers adviser (if you have one), who might suggest you sit a timed practice test prior to your actual test day. Such practice is available nowadays in most universities to give you some feedback on your performance, so you know what you should work on before the actual test.
- Acquainting and familiarizing yourself with what is required, by hard work and practice prior to the test, will help you to improve your performance.
- Avoid being nervous; believe in yourself.
- At the beginning of each test, you are given a couple of examples to ensure you know what you are required to do. Don't hesitate to ask the assessor to clarify the instructions and remove any ambiguity.

- The best way to choose alternatives in multiple choices is to eliminate all wrong answers and use your judgement to choose the best answer from the remaining ones.
- To meet the test requirements, particular care should be taken with the way you record your answers on the answer sheet. Apply the rules exactly. If you are asked to cross the chosen box, you should do exactly that; anything else might be marked as incorrect even though you might have answered the question correctly.
- Always do your rough work on separate scraps of paper and don't mark your question book or the answer sheet unnecessarily.
- Work as quickly and accurately as you can and avoid taking too long over a question; however, if you still have time left, go back to sort it out.

1

Psychometric tests for IT and finance

Diagrammatic reasoning using the alphabet

In this test you are shown a number of diagrams representing an input → transformation → output process in which the input is altered by rules depending on commands, which are represented by symbols. Your task is to identify the rule represented by each symbol, based on the information in the diagram, and to apply these rules to the input data you are given. Different rules may be used for the same symbol in different diagrams. Therefore, consider each diagram on its own and work out what rule each symbol stands for; don't generalize the rules for the whole test. No two different symbols have the same rules in the same diagram. As a rule of thumb always follow the arrow for input and output for every path independently. Table 1.1 shows some of the common rules used in alphabetic diagrammatic reasoning. It is only to give an idea about what to expect. However, other possibilities are left to your imagination.

Table 1.1 Some common alphabetic diagrammatic reasoning rules

	Input	Output	Comment
1.	ABCD	ABC	Delete right
2.	ABCD	BCD	Delete left
3.	ABCD	ABD	Delete third from left
4.	ABCD	ACD	Delete second from left
5.	ABCD	DABC	Last is first
6.	ABCD	BCDA	First is last
7.	ABCD	ABDC	Exchange the position of the last two characters
8.	ABCD	ACBD	Exchange the position of the middle two characters
9.	ABCD	DCBA	Move sequence to the front
10.	ABCD	DBCA	Exchange the first and last
11.	ABCD	ABCDF	Add a new character F to the sequence
12.	ABCD	AABCD	Add similar character to the first
13.	ABCD	ABCE	Change the last character to the next letter in the alphabet
14.	ABCD	CDAB	Exchange every two characters from left to right

Tips

Consider the example shown in Figure 1.1 and follow the rules as one way to solve the problem:

- Identify the shortest path by following only one input and output path. In Figure 1.1 we have three paths; path 1 and path 2 are the shortest and path 3 is the longest.
- Identify all the identical symbols; if identical symbols appear in one diagram, they must obey the same rules.
- Work out the shortest path rules, ie path 1 and path 2, using Table 1.1 as your guide, as shown in Figure 1.2. As you can see, once you have figured out the rules for one symbol you can apply the same rules straightaway to other similar symbols in the same diagram. By doing this you will save time.
- In any one diagram, two different symbols do not have the same rules.
- Finally, go back to the longest path, path 3; as you can see, you are left to find out the rules for only one symbol, #. Again, consider the common rules introduced in Table 1.1 in conjunction with the other symbols as shown in Figure 1.2.

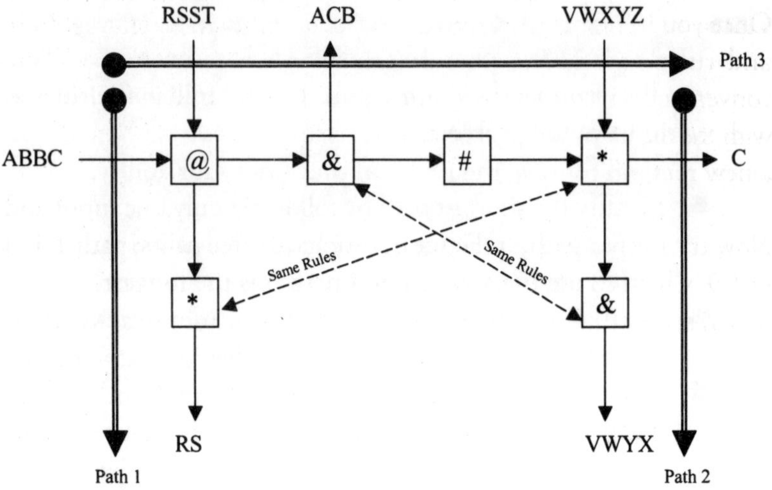

Figure 1.1 Illustrates the three paths

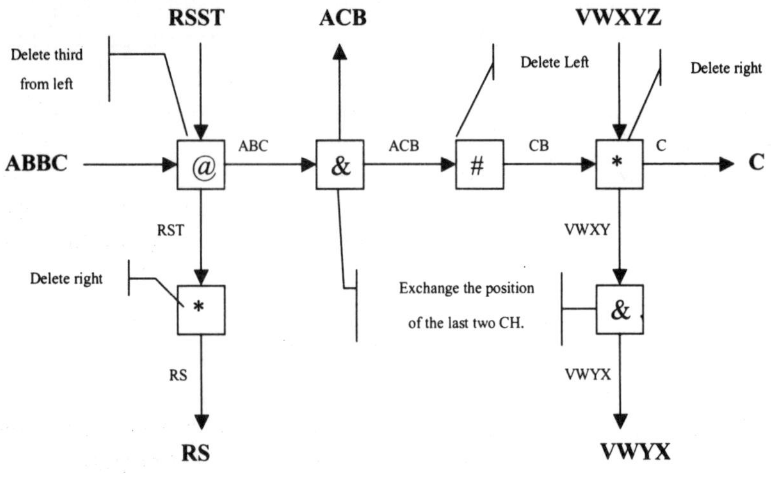

Figure 1.2 Shows step-by-step solution

Once you have mastered the basics, try to define your own symbols and rules and devise new diagrams to suit your ability and convenience. However, I am sure that as you become more familiar with the diagrams you will be able to create your own way and devise a new method to solve the problem that suits your ability.

Now try the following practice questions, as shown in Figures 1.3 to 1.9, which contain 40 questions. Marking your answers on scrap paper, see how many questions you can do in 30 minutes.

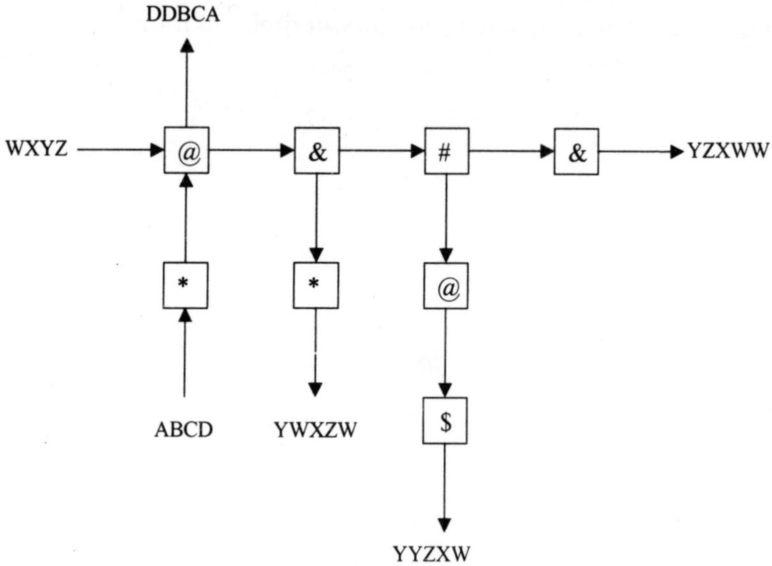

Figure 1.3

1. WXYZ → [@] → [@] → ?

2. JKLMN → [#] → [&] → ?

3. ABCD → [*] → [?] → [#] → DBCA

4. JKLMN → [*] → [@] → ?

5. LMNO → [?] → [*] → [#] → LNMLO

6. ABCD → [?] → [?] → [#] → DBA

Questions for 1.3

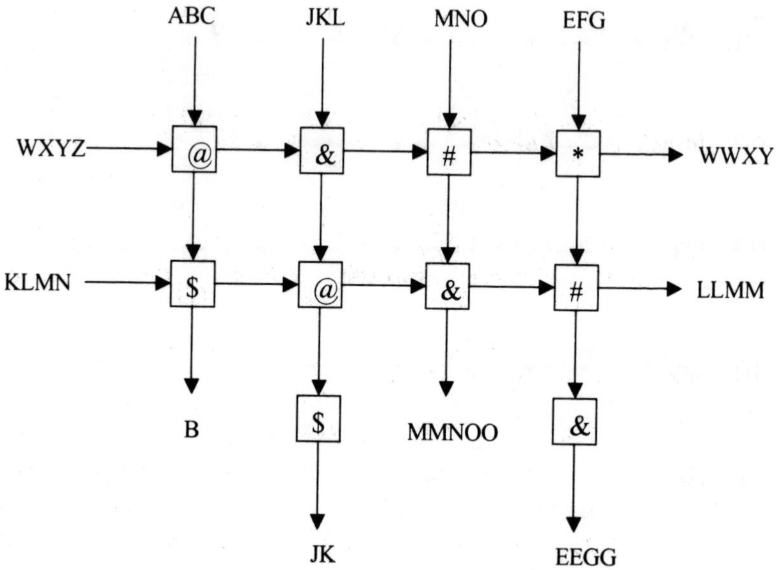

Figure 1.4

7. ABC → [@] → [#] → ?

8. MOP → [?] → [&] → [#] → MMOO

9. EFGH → [?] → [?] → [*] → EEEFH

10. ABC → [&] → [*] → ?

11. OOPP → [@] → [?] → [#] → OPP

12. JKLMN → [*] → [@] → ?

Questions for 1.4

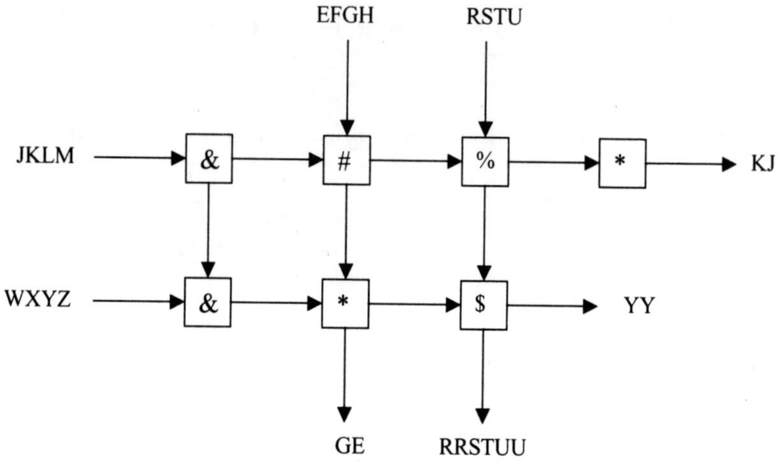

Figure 1.5

13. ABCD → [&] → [?] → ABCC

14. ABCD → [#] → [%] → [?] → BCA

15. ABCD → [*] → [#] → [&] → ?

16. ABCD → [%] → [?] → [*] → BCDD

17. ? → [$] → [#] → ACBAD

18. BBA → [$] → [#] → [?] → BBAA

Questions for 1.5

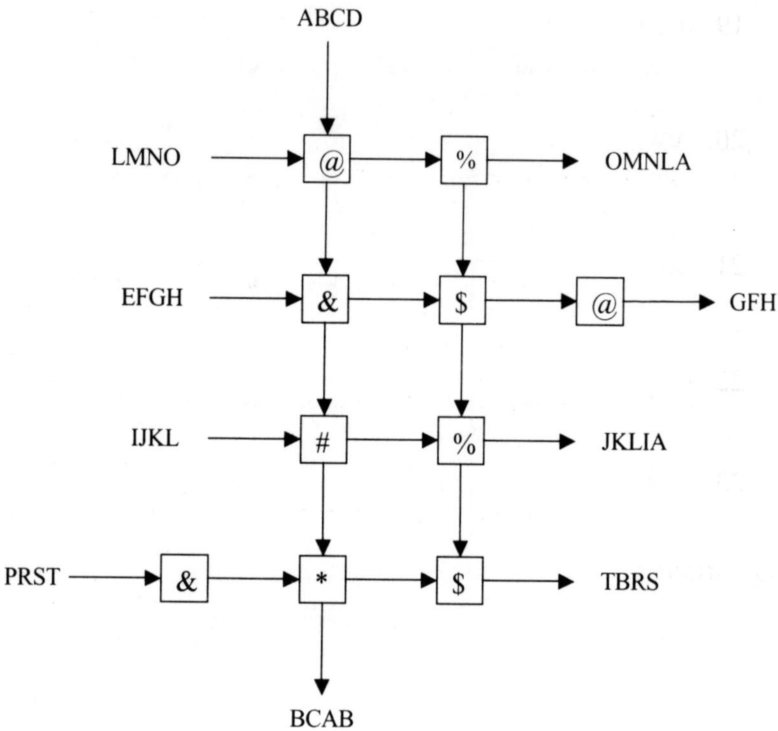

Figure 1.6

19. LMNO → % → * → ?

20. VWXY → # → $ → % → ?

21. ABCD → & → * → @ → ?

22. ? → $ → # → QRS

23. ANA → $ → # → # → ?

Questions for 1.6

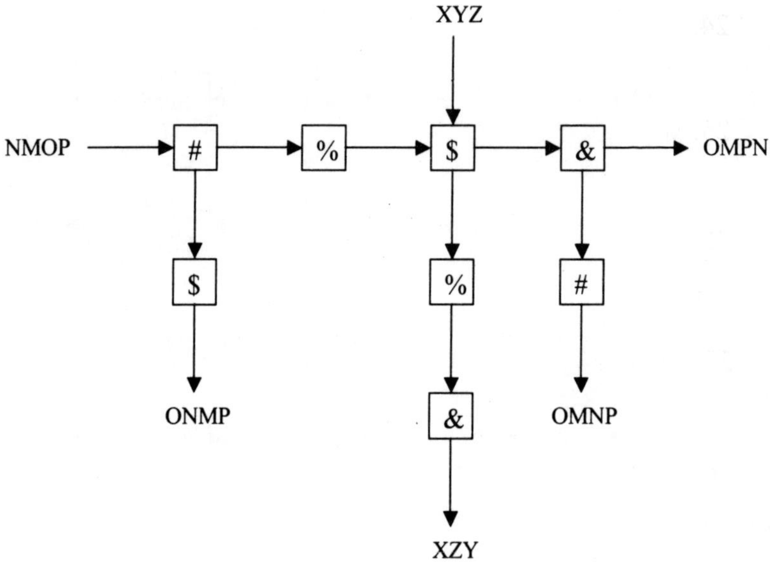

Figure 1.7

24. ABC → [$] → [#] → ?

25. MNOO → [?] → [&] → [#] → NOOM

26. XYZZ → [#] → [&] → [%] → ?

27. POQR → [$] → [?] → [#] → PORQ

28. OOPP → [%] → [?] → [#] → OPPO

29. JKLM → [&] → [$] → ?

Questions for 1.7

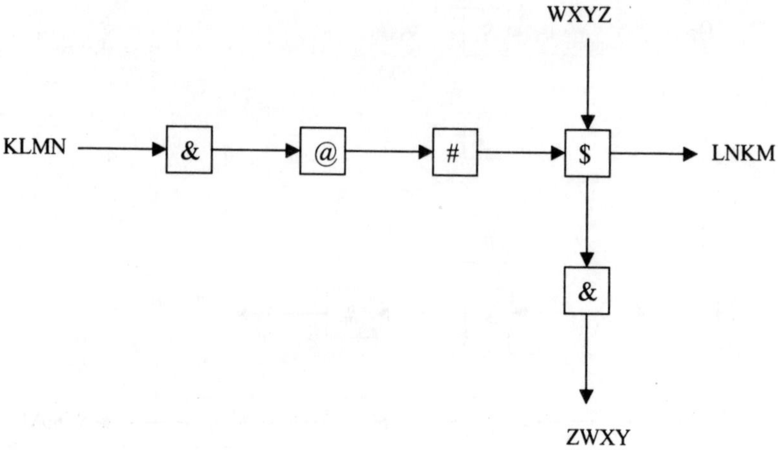

Figure 1.8

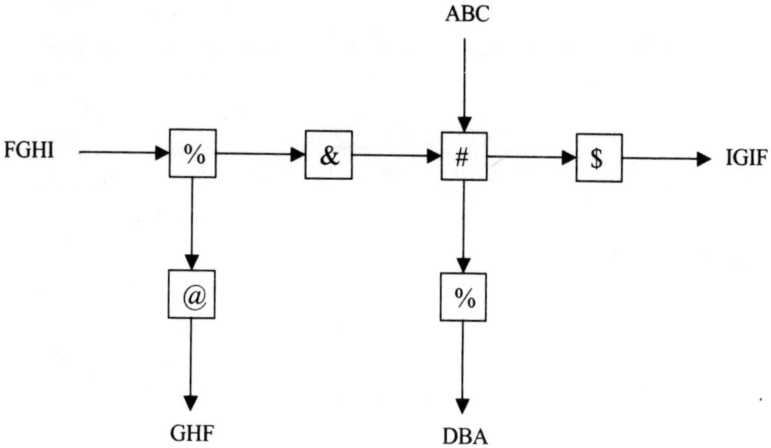

Figure 1.9

30. LMN → [$] → [#] → ?

31. POLO → [@] → [&] → ?

32. RST → [#] → [?] → RST

33. POQR → [$] → [&] → [#] → ?

34. ABCD → [&] → [?] → [#] → CBDA

35. JKLM → [&] → [#] → ?

Questions for 1.8

36. FGHI → [$] → [#] → ?

37. QRST → [?] → [&] → [%] → SRT

38. VWXY → [#] → [&] → [@] → ?

39. OOTR → [$] → [&] → [?] → ROTO

40. OOPP → [%] → [?] → [#] → OPP

Questions for 1.9

Diagrammatic reasoning using shapes

In this case you are shown a number of diagrams in which a shape (in a square box) is altered by a command represented by a symbol (we use similar symbols as before; however, they are put in circles rather than squares). Table 1.2 shows some of the common rules used, just to give you an idea of what you should expect. Be aware that these are not the only possibilities.

Table 1.2

	Shape	Altered	Comment
1.	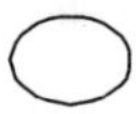	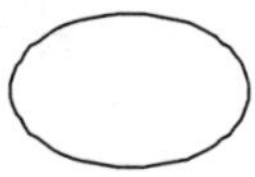	Change of size
2.	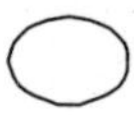		Change of colour
3.	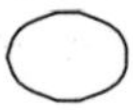	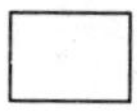	Change of shape
4.	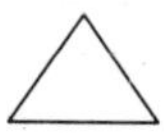	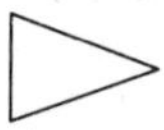	Rotate to any angle
5.	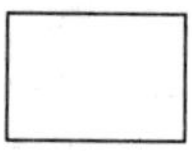	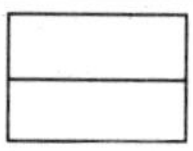	Add horizontal line
6.	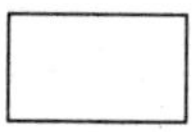	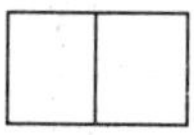	Add vertical line
7.			Turn only the colour upside down

Tips

Consider the example shown in Figure 1.10 and follow the simple rules below as one way to solve the problem:

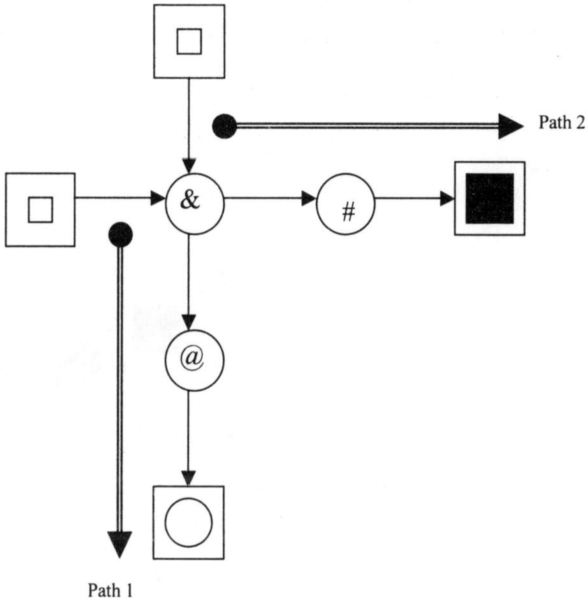

Figure 1.10 Shows the three paths

- Identify the shortest path by following only one input and output path. In Figure 1.10 we have only two equal paths to consider at the same time. Follow the rules represented by each symbol and see the solution in Figure 1.11.
- Identify similar symbols; since they are in one diagram, they must obey the same rules. However, a symbol may well have a different meaning in another Figure; therefore avoid generalization in your test.

- In any one diagram, two different symbols do not have the same rules.
- The same symbol may appear twice in a sequence in a single Figure. The symbol may, for example, convert the shape from square to circle, but the second time the same symbol converts it back again, which is different from the rules used in diagrammatic reasoning using the alphabet.

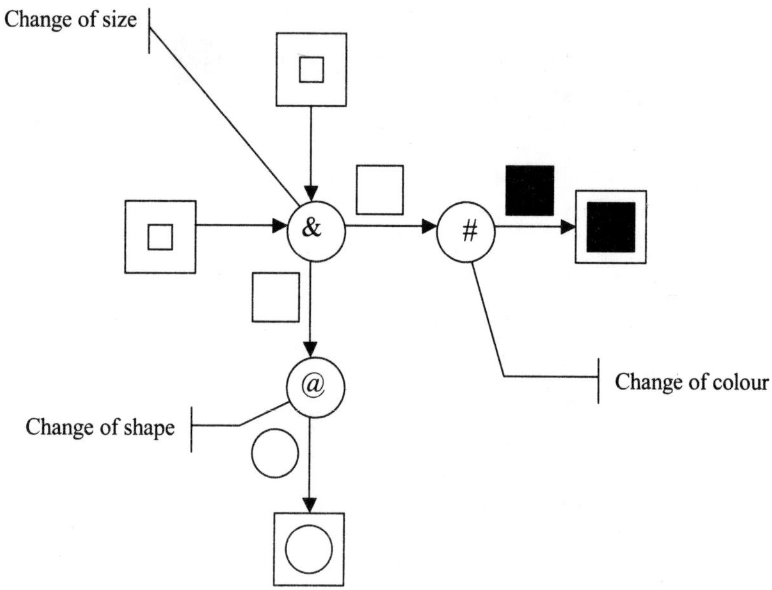

Figure 1.11 Shows the solution of the above example

However, I am sure that as you become more familiar with the diagrams you will be able to create your own way and devise a new method to solve the problem that suits your ability.

Now try the following practice questions as shown in Figures 1.12 to 1.15, which contain 24 questions. Mark your answers on scrap paper and see how many questions you can do in 15 minutes.

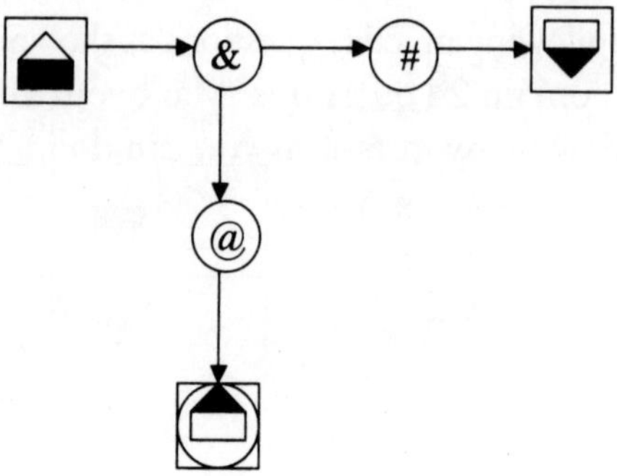

Figure 1.12

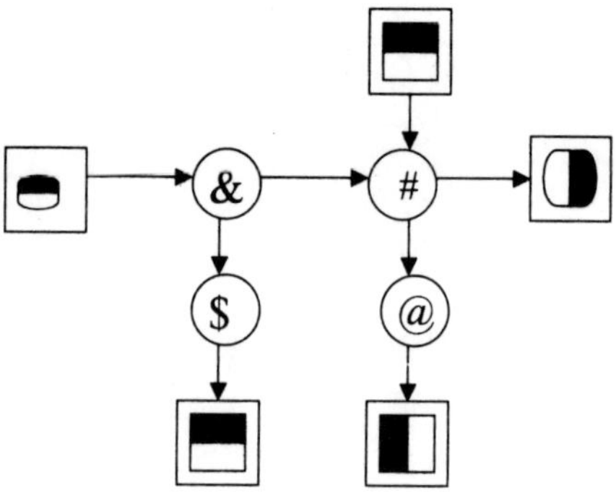

Figure 1.13

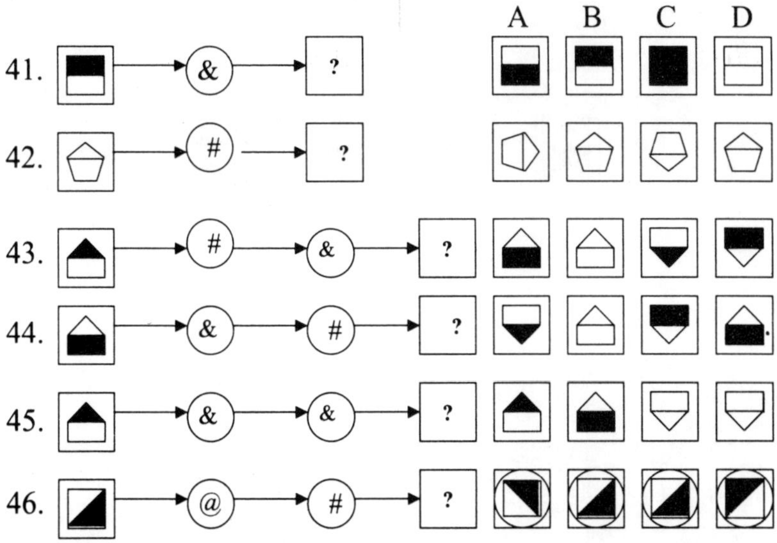

Questions for 1.12

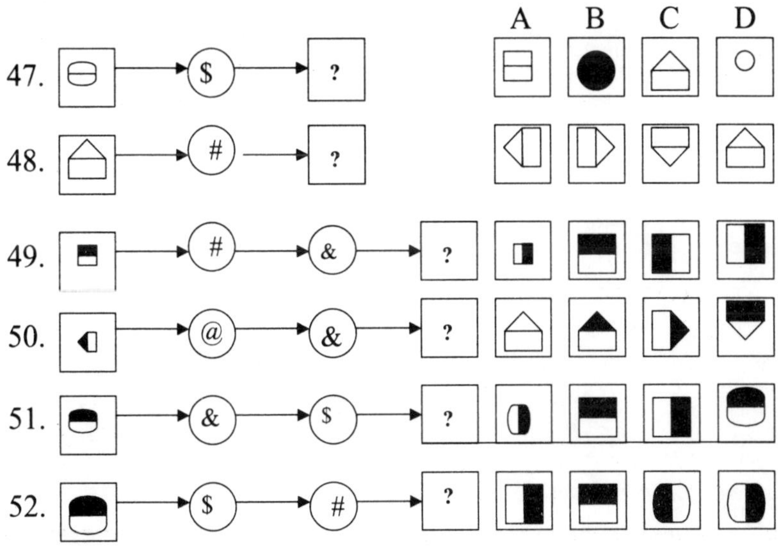

Questions for 1.13

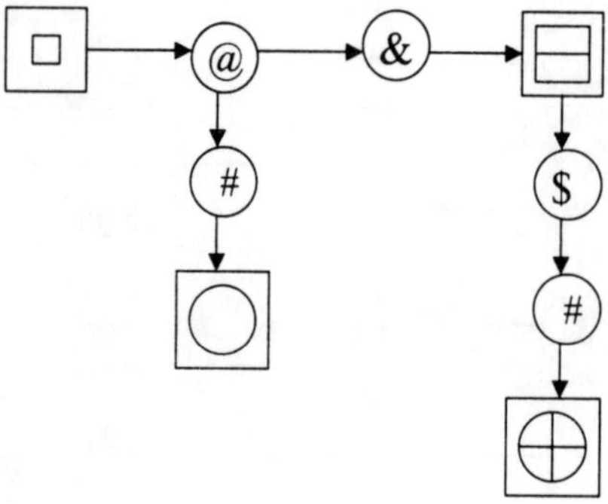

Figure 1.14

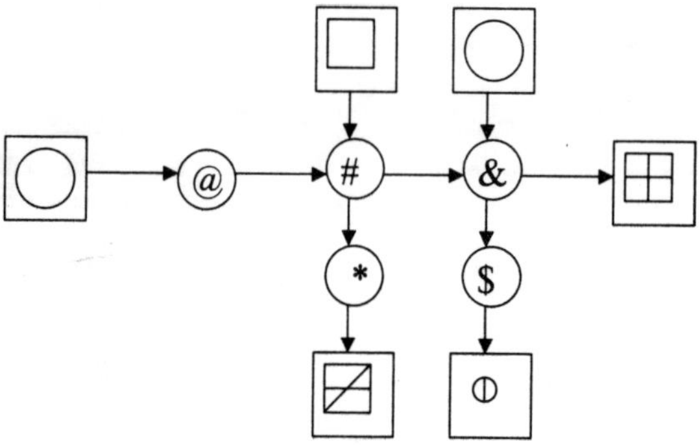

Figure 1.15

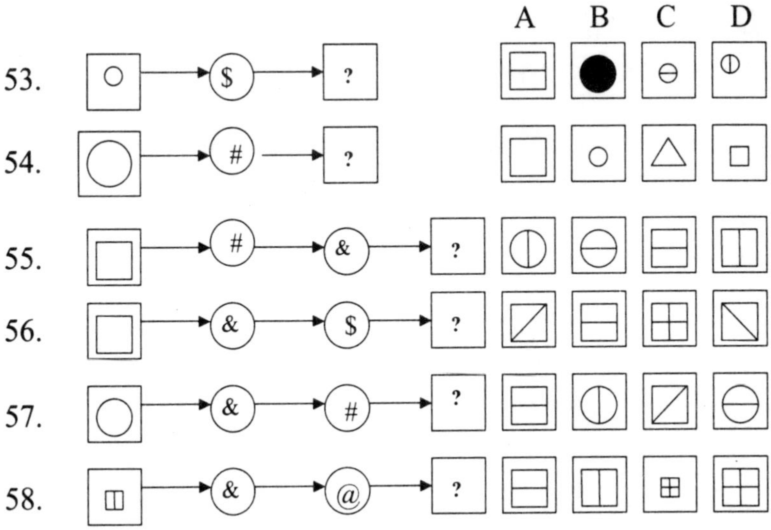

Questions for 1.14

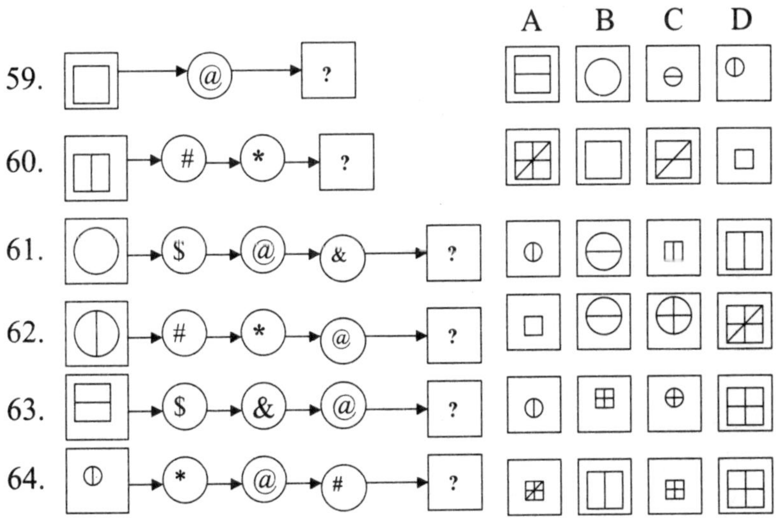

Questions for 1.15

Diagrammatic reasoning using control process boxes

The test consists of four control process or transformation boxes and a control flow arrow inside a rectangle. Each box is responsible for a certain process for changing a shape. These processes, from top to bottom, are defined in Figure 1.16.

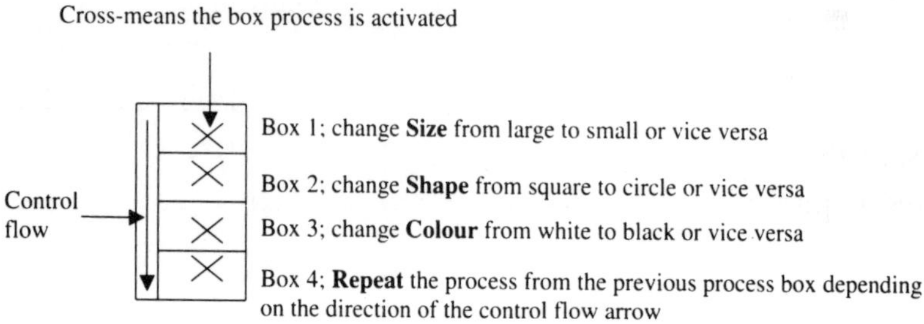

Figure 1.16 The order of the four control process boxes and the transformations they apply

The order of the process boxes, from box 1 to box 4, is constant throughout the test. The box is activated (enabled) only when it has a cross inside; otherwise the operation of that particular box is ignored. In other words, all transformation of the data flow to it is ignored. To trigger a process box is to activate it (to put a cross in it) so that it carries out its transformation process. The control flow arrow is responsible for the direction of the transformation process, either from box 1 to box 4 or from box 4 to box 1, as illustrated in the example in Figure 1.17.

As you can see, the output of the development of the shape, ie a square in this case, is dissimilar, even though we have activated the same process boxes. This is due to the direction of the control flow arrow.

Tips

- Identify the direction of the control flow arrow. This will help you to decide whether to process the boxes from top to bottom or vice versa.
- Pay special attention to box 4 (the repeat box); if activated (crossed) it can repeat the process of either box 3 (change colour) or box 1 (change size), depending on the direction of the control arrow.
- Bear in mind that an uncrossed box means an inactivated process and should be ignored.

Start the test when you have understood the basic concept of the test requirements, using Figure 1.16 as your guide. Diagrammatic

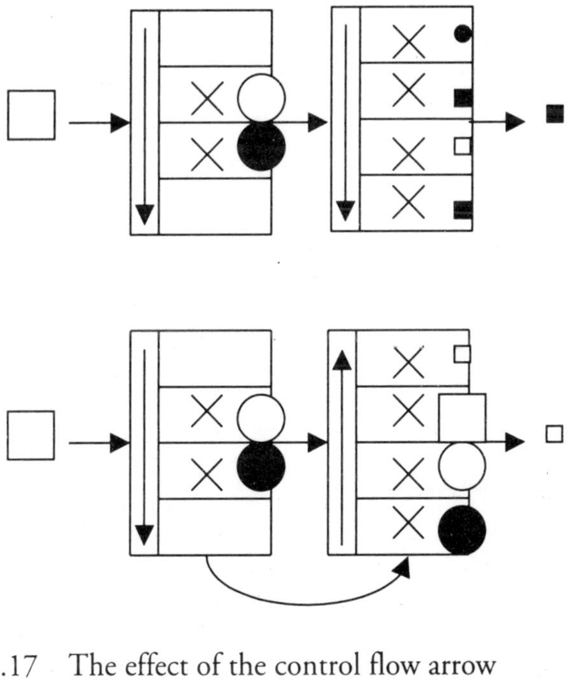

Figure 1.17 The effect of the control flow arrow

reasoning using control process boxes consists of test 1 and test 2 each with 20 questions (40 questions in total). In test 1, you have to decide the least number of process boxes that should be activated (crossed) in order to achieve the output transformation shape. In test 2, you have to select one output transformation shape from four given choices, ie A, B, C and D. In both tests the last 10 questions are more difficult because the control arrow takes different directions. You have 25 minutes to complete both tests.

Test 1

1.

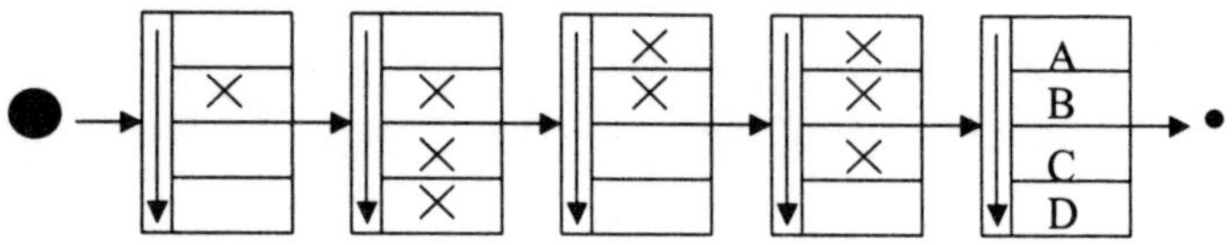

2.

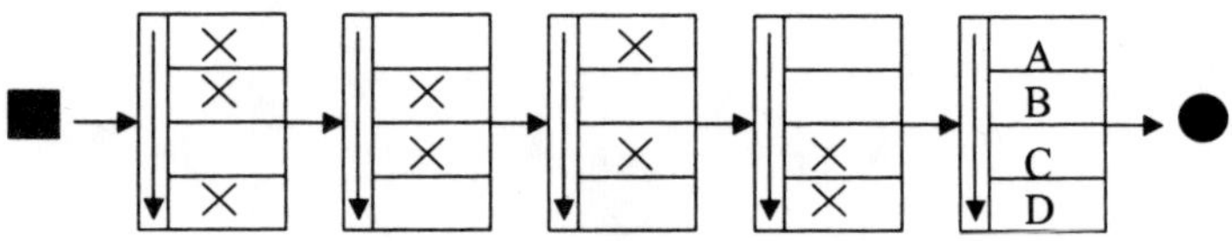

3.

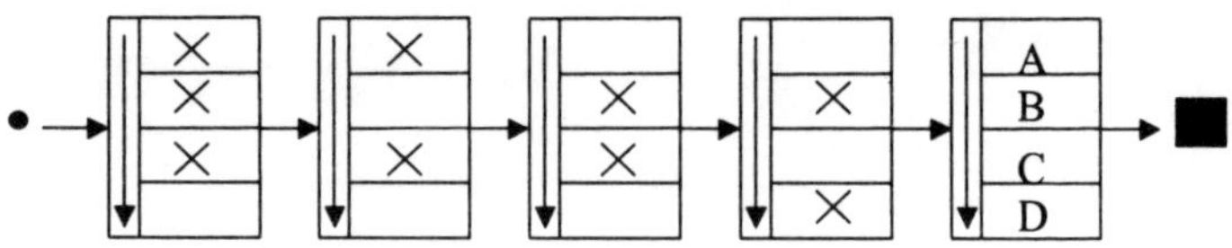

4.

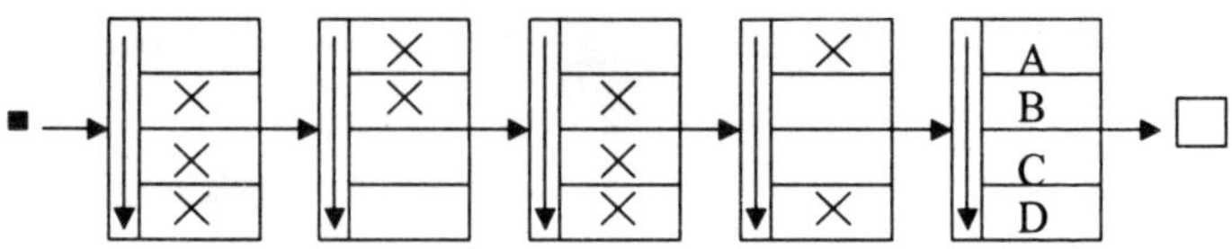

5.

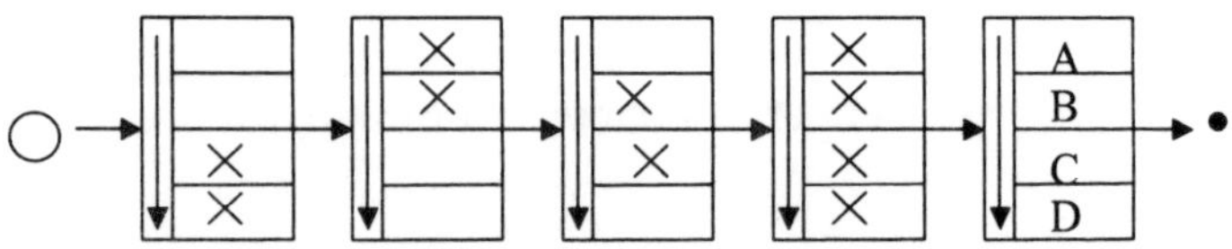

6.

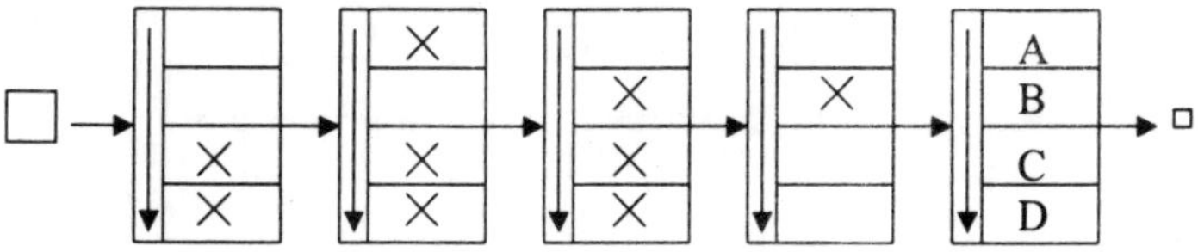

7.

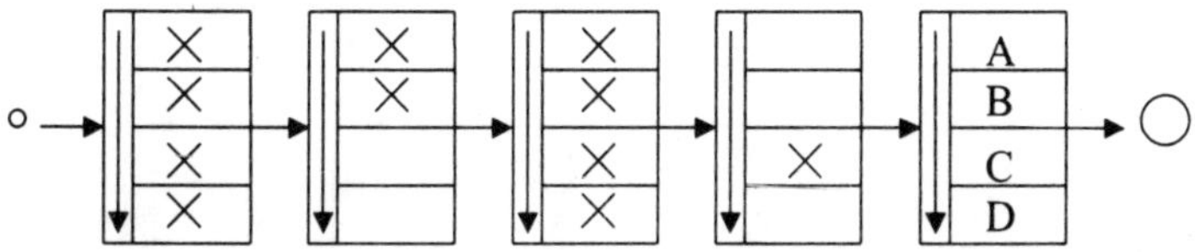

8.

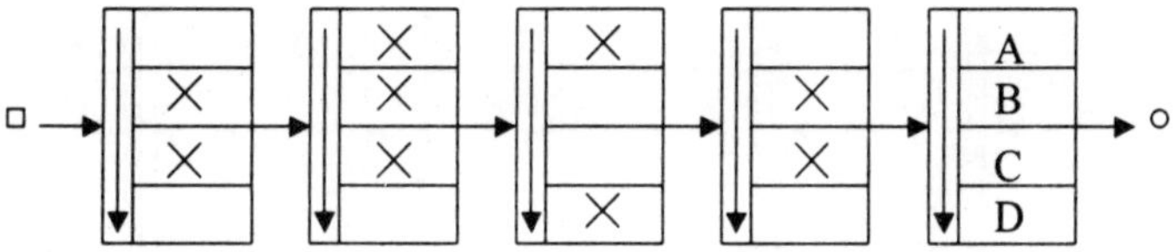

9.

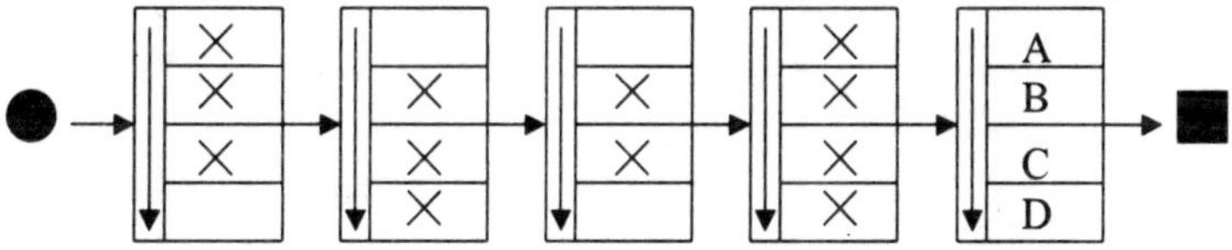

10.

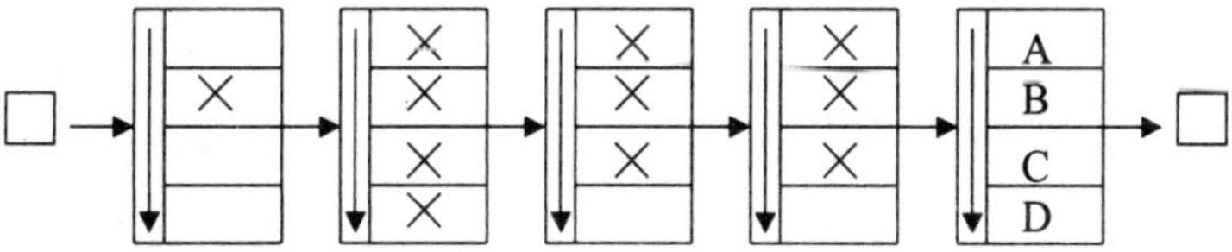

11.

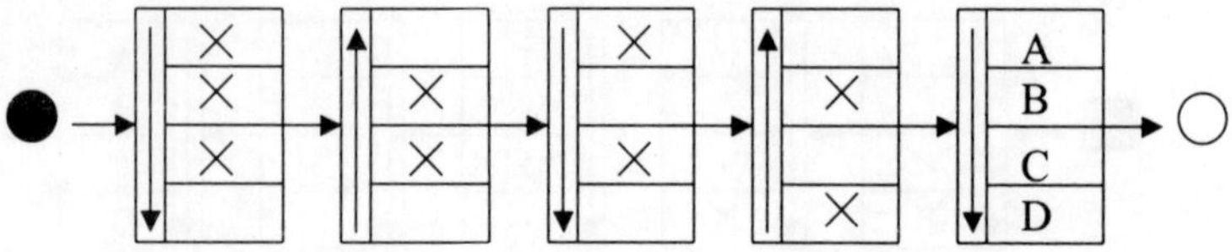

12.

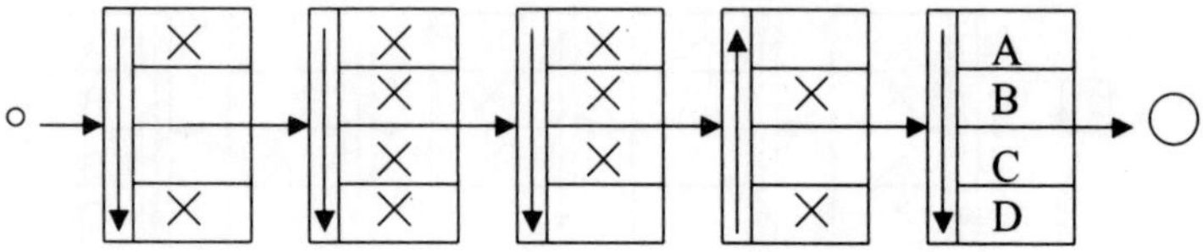

13.

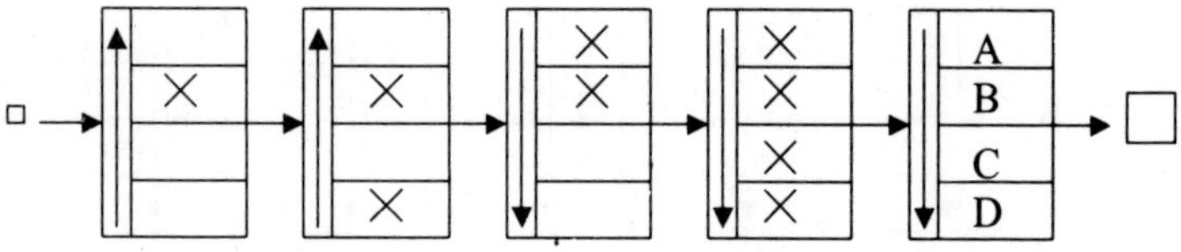

14.

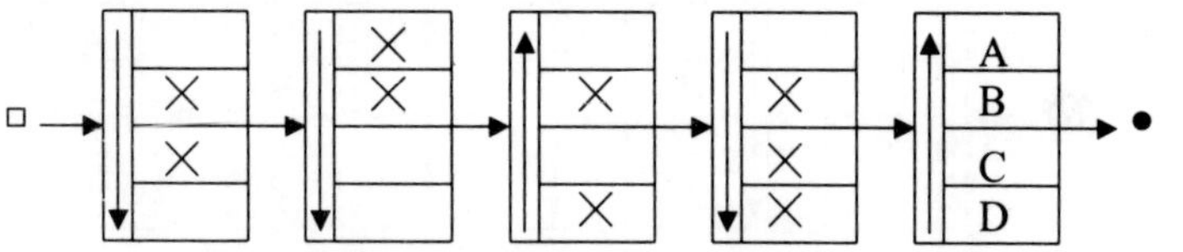

15.

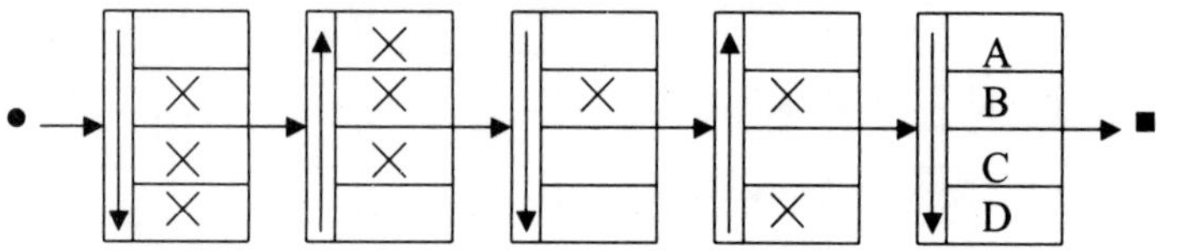

16.

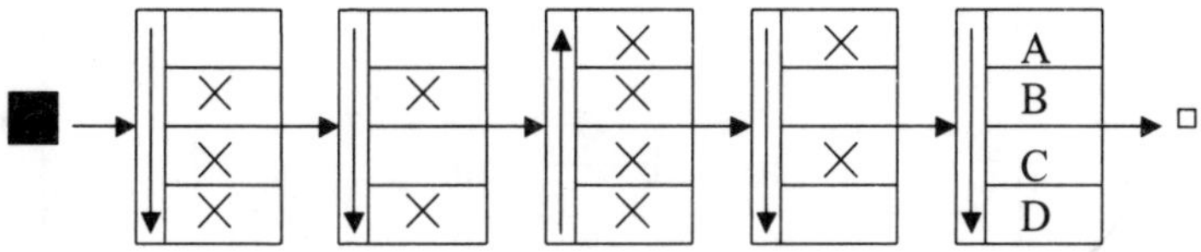

17.

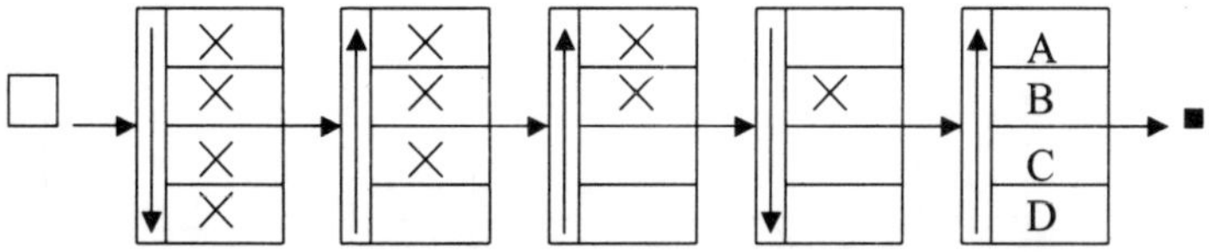

18.

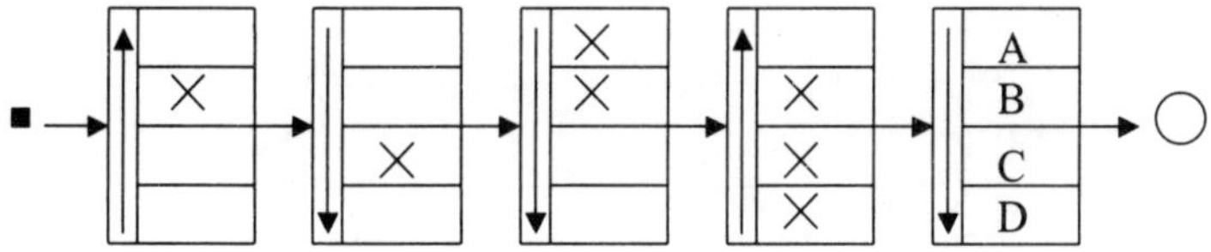

19.

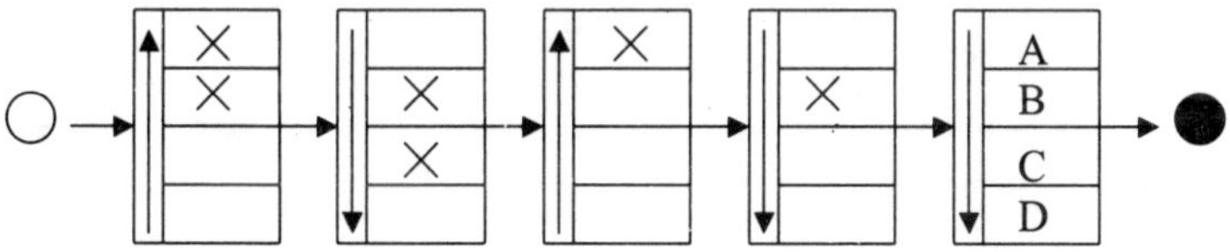

20.

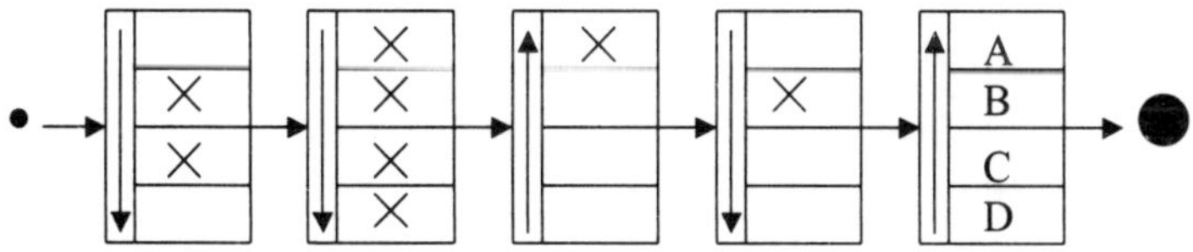

Test 2

1.

A B C D

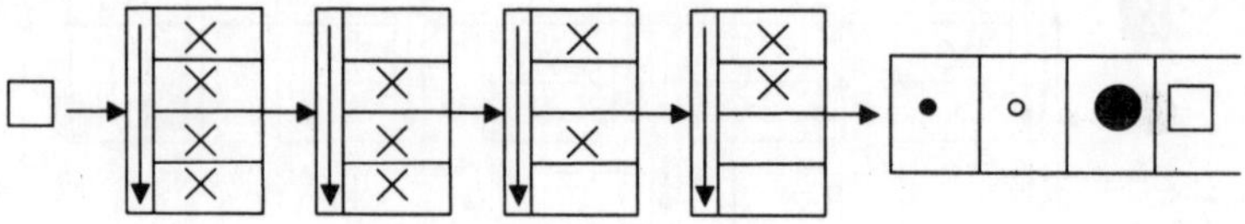

2.

A B C D

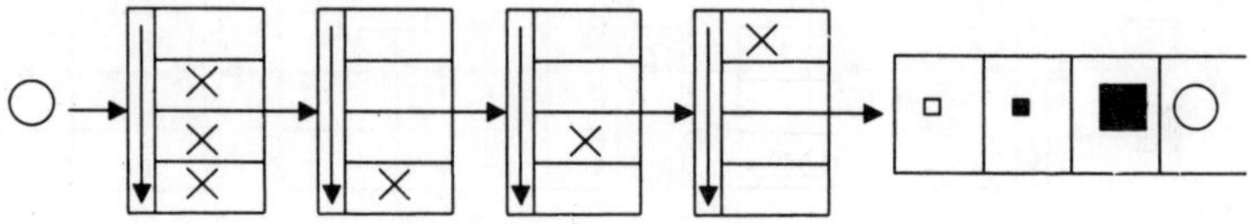

3.

A B C D

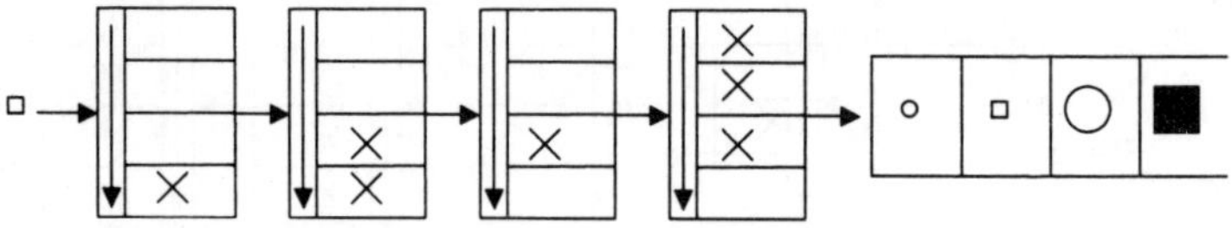

4.

A B C D

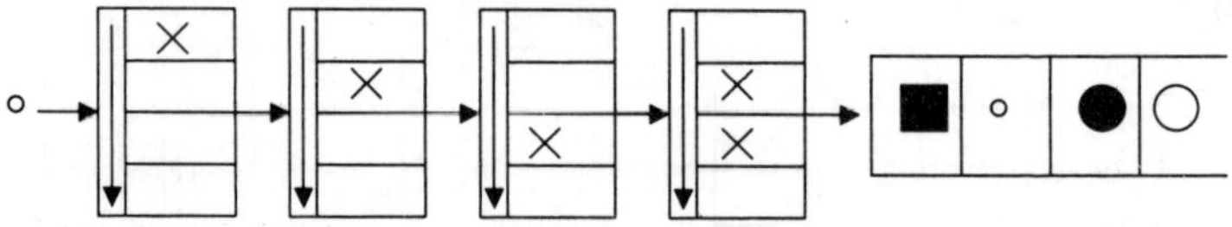

5.

A B C D

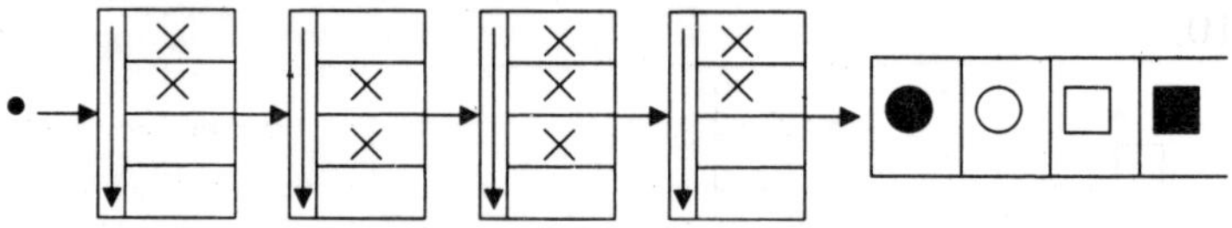

6.

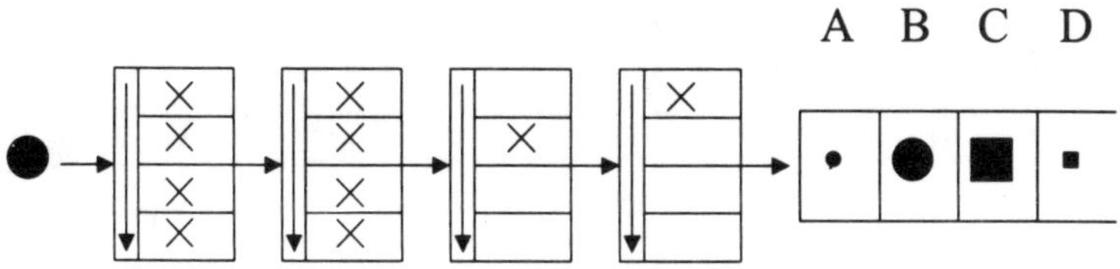

7.

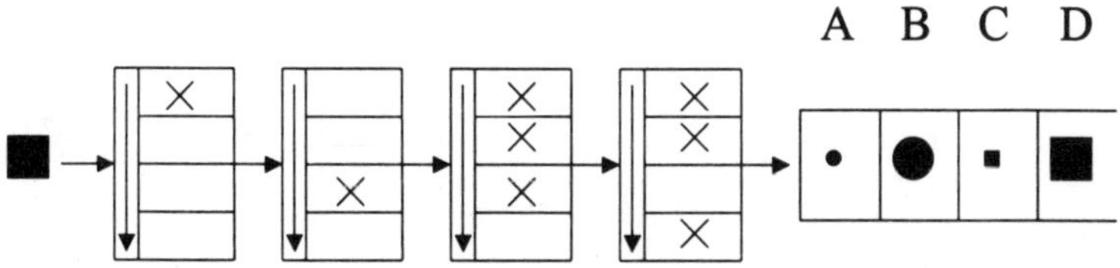

8.

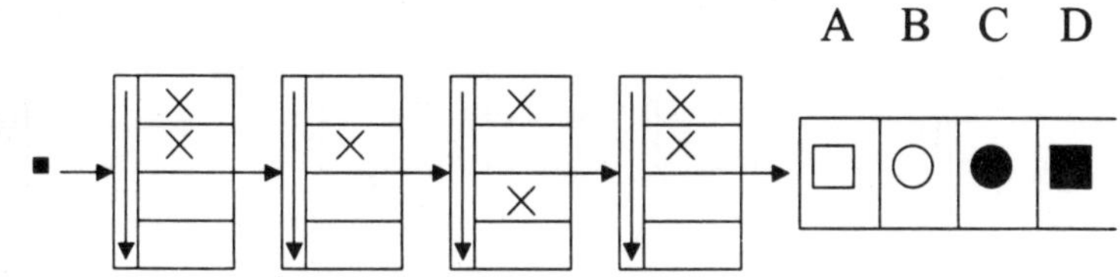

9.

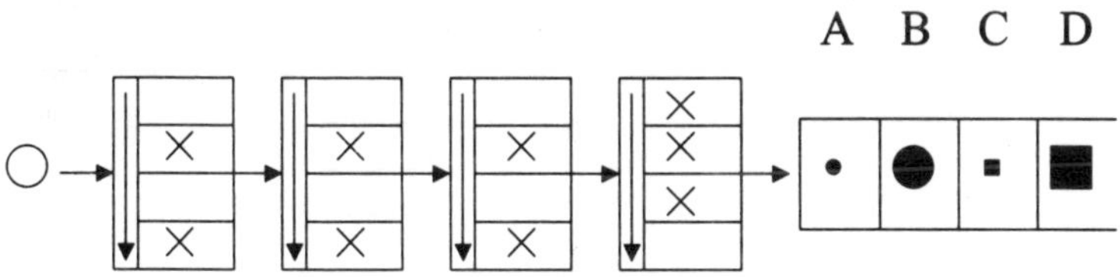

10.

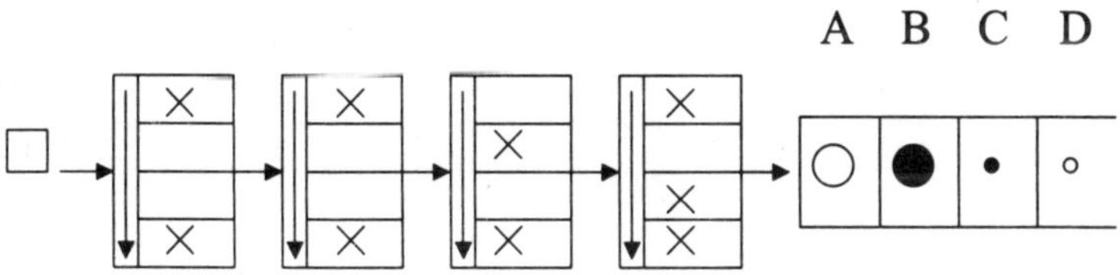

11.

A B C D

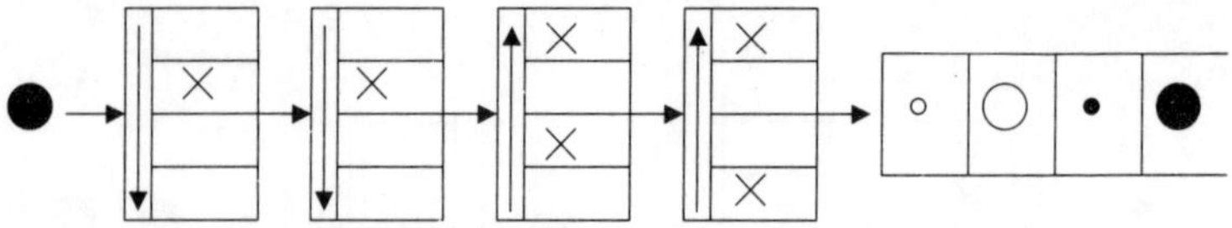

12.

A B C D

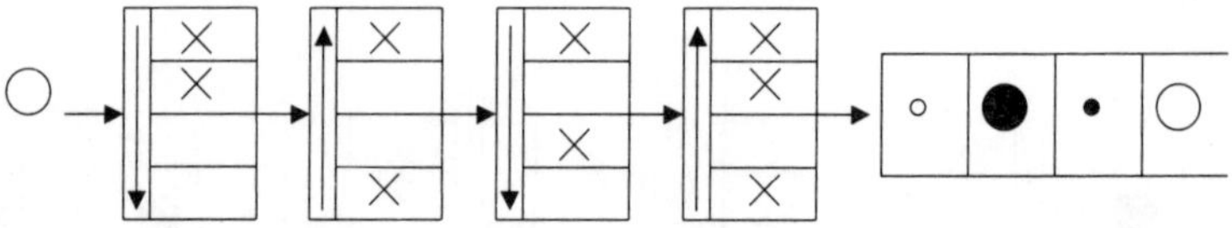

13.

A B C D

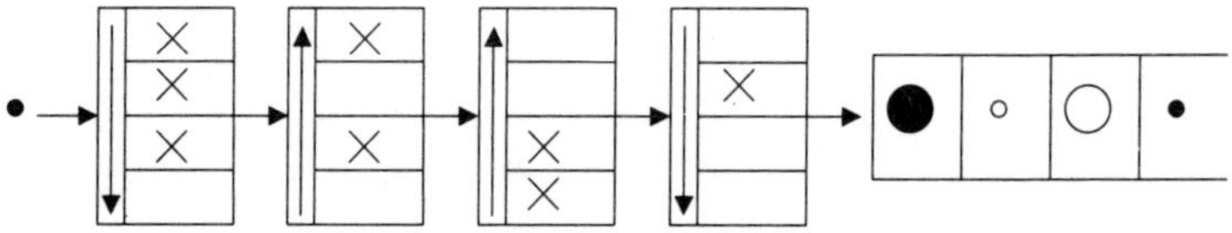

14.

A B C D

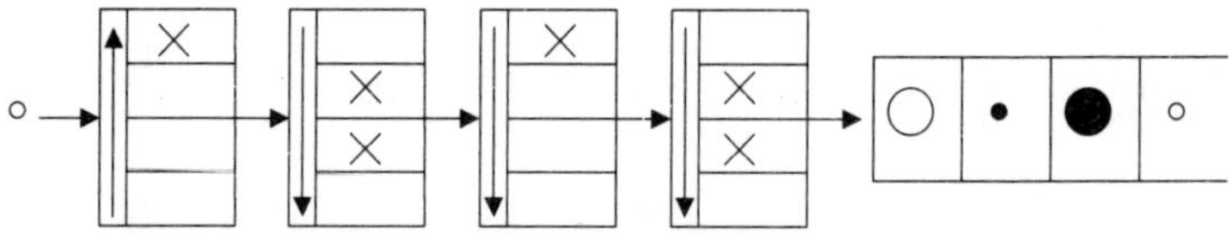

15.

A B C D

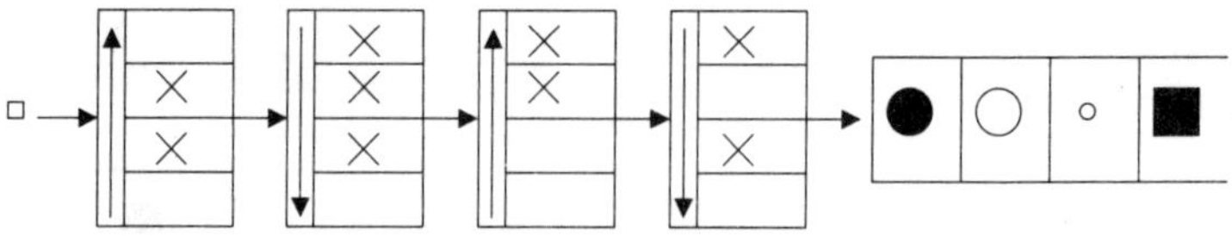

16. A B C D

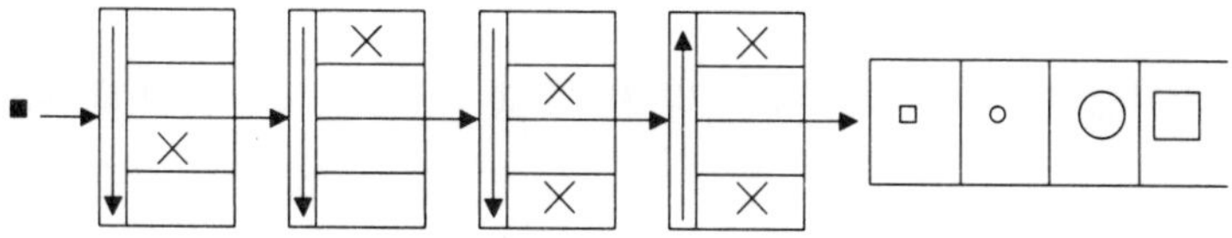

17. A B C D

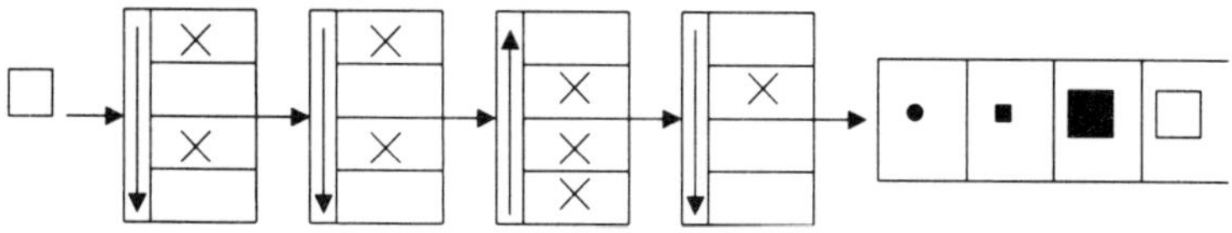

18. A B C D

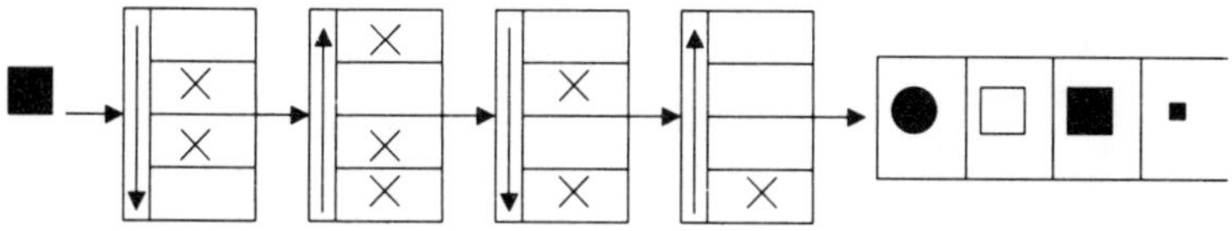

19. A B C D

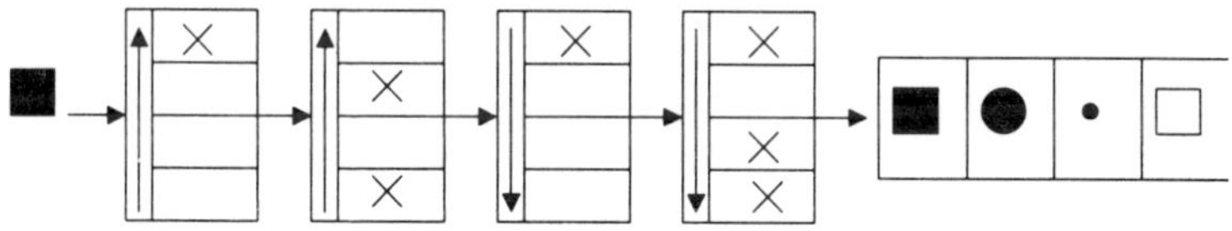

20. A B C D

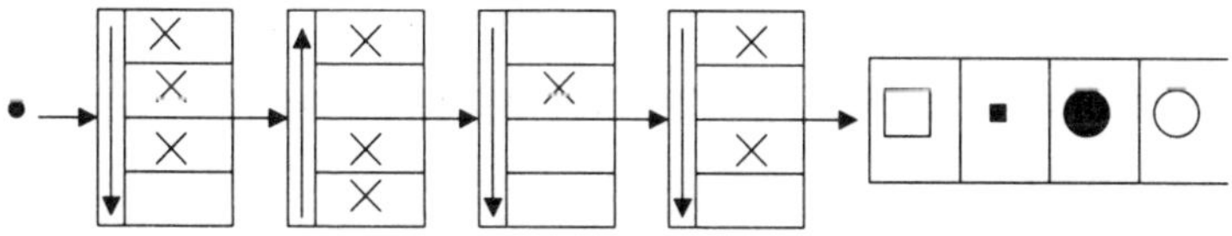

Answers to practice exercises

Diagrammatic reasoning using the alphabet

1. WWWXYZ
2. NMLJK
3. #
4. NNKLMJ
5. @
6. &, $
7. ABB
8. @
9. &, &
10. AAC
11. $
12. JKL
13. $
14. *
15. D
16. $
17. DCBA
18. #
19. BLMNOA
20. VWXYA
21. DBCB
22. QRS
23. NAA
24. CBA
25. %
26. XZZY
27. &
28. $
29. JKLM
30. LMN

31. LPOO
32. $
33. QRPO
34. @
35. KLMJ
36. GHIG
37. @
38. VWX
39. %
40. @

Solutions for diagrammatic reasoning tests using the alphabet

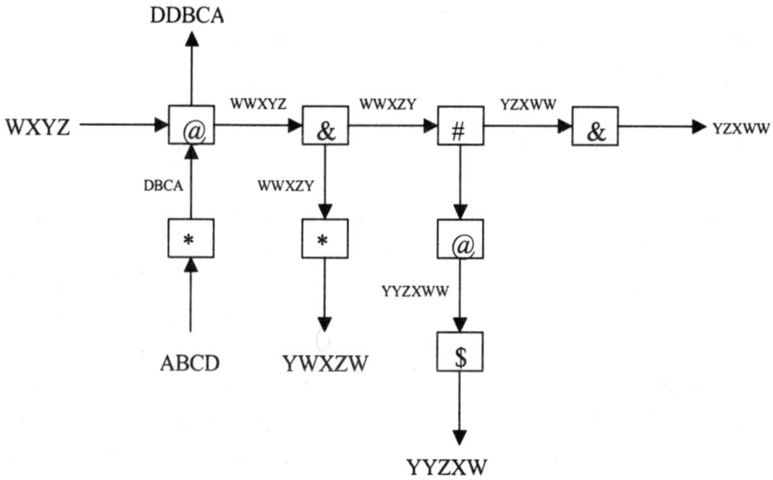

Figure 1.3 Solution

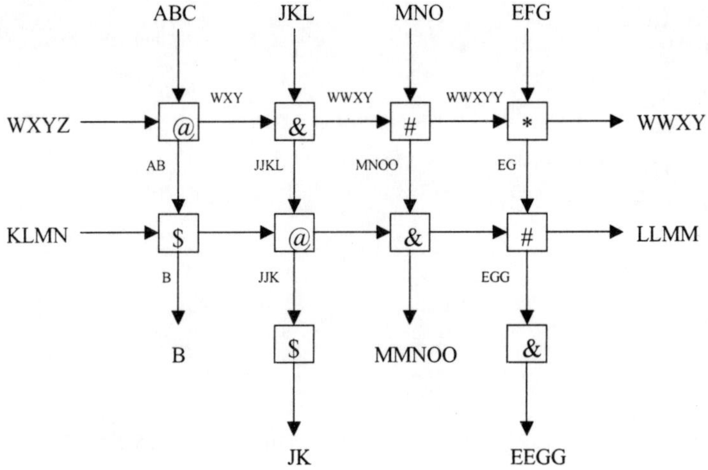

Figure 1.4 Solution

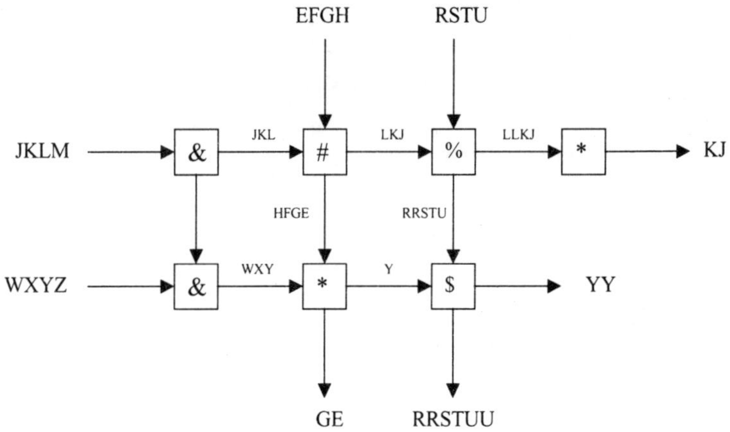

Figure 1.5 Solution

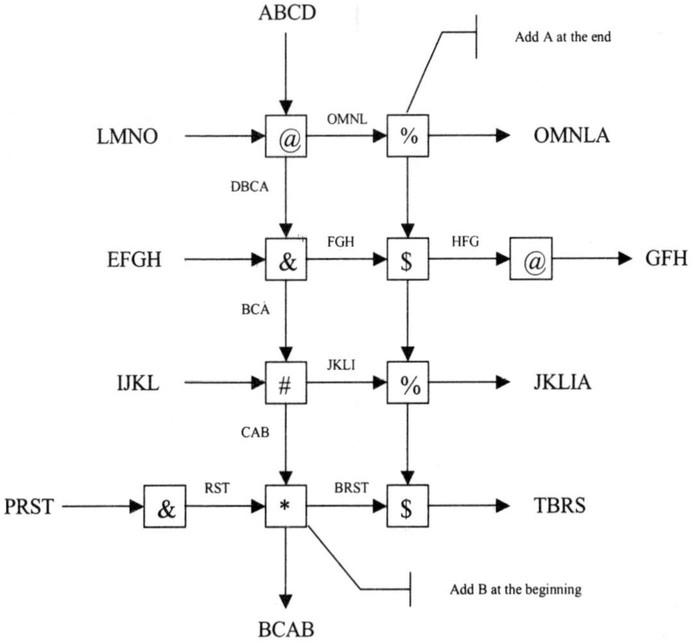

Figure 1.6 Solution

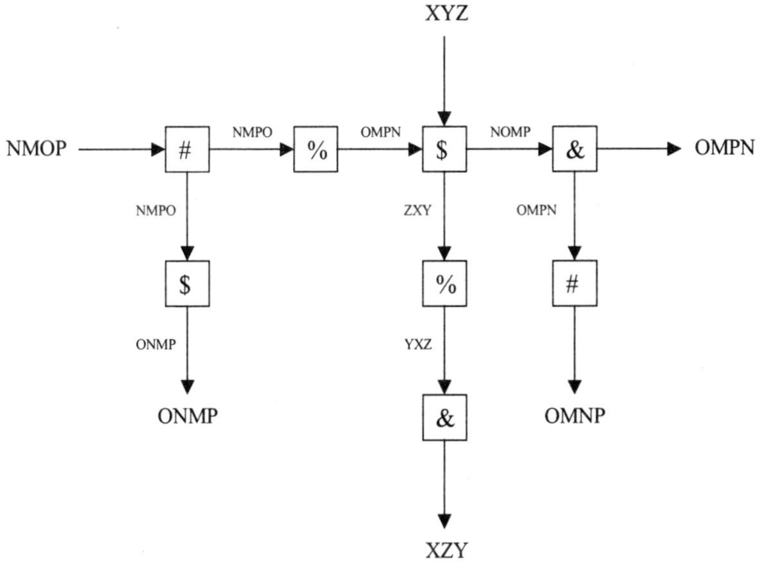

Figure 1.7 Solution

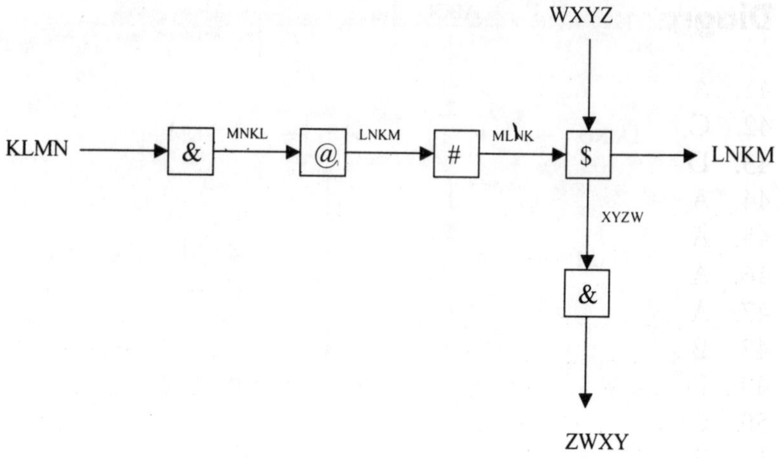

Figure 1.8 Solution

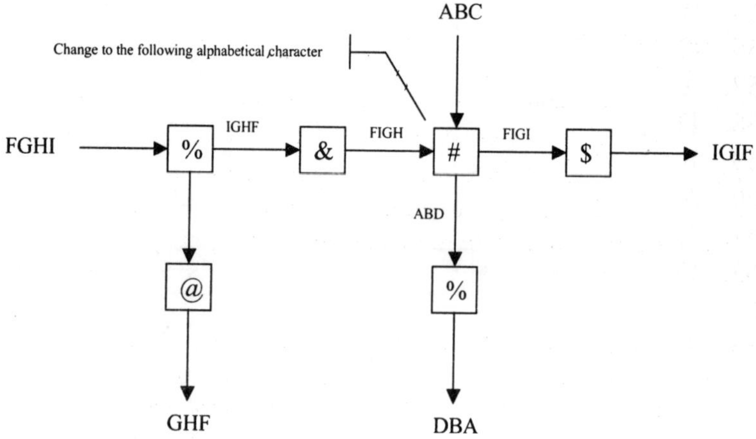

Figure 1.9 Solution

Diagrammatic reasoning using shapes

41. A
42. C
43. D
44. A
45. A
46. A
47. A
48. B
49. D
50. C
51. B
52. A
53. D
54. A
55. B
56. C
57. A
58. D
59. B
60. A
61. C
62. D
63. C
64. A

Solutions for diagrammatic reasoning tests using shapes

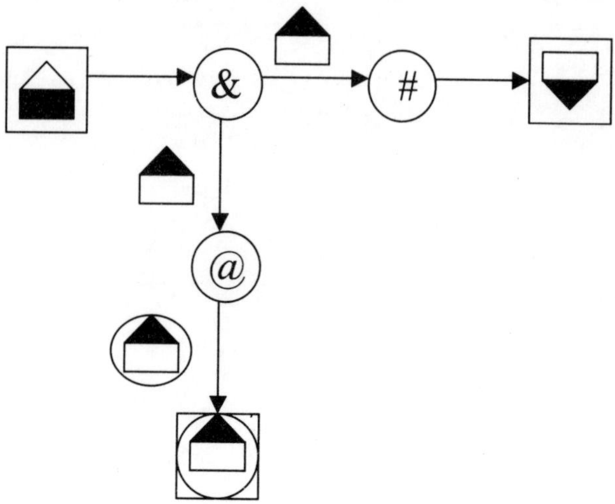

Figure 1.12 Solution

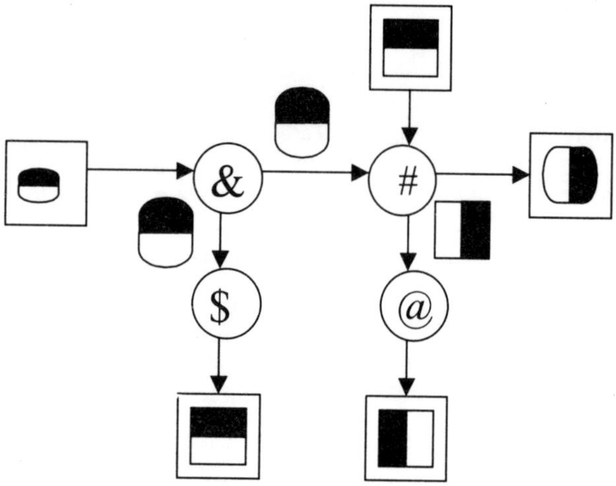

Figure 1.13 Solution

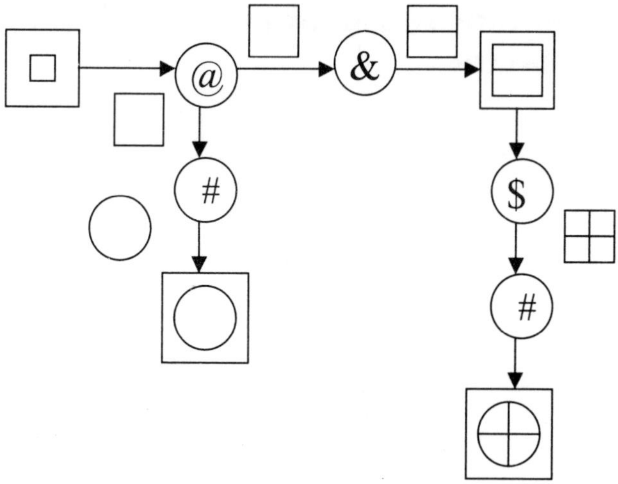

Figure 1.14 Solution

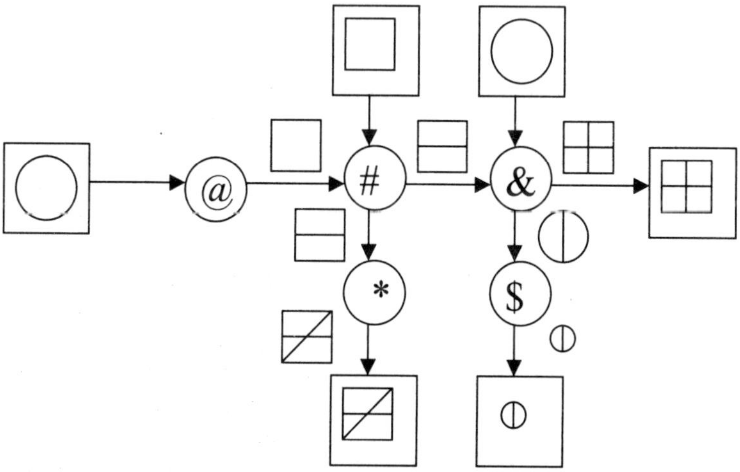

Figure 1.15 Solution

Diagrammatic reasoning using control process boxes

Test 1

1. A&C
2. B
3. A&C
4. A&B&C
5. A&B
6. D
7. B&C
8. C
9. B
10. A
11. B
12. B&C
13. A
14. A&B
15. A&B&C
16. A&B&C
17. D
18. C
19. B
20. A&B&C

Solution for diagrammatic reasoning tests using control process boxes: test 1

1.

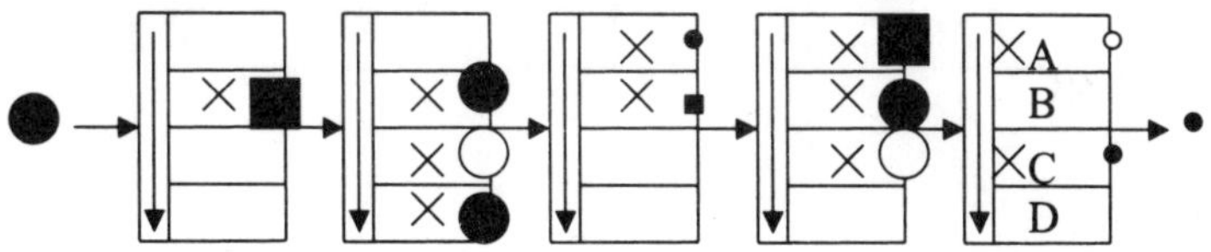

2.

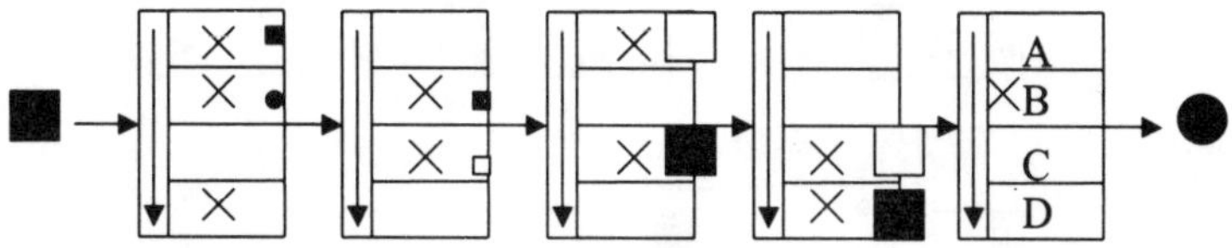

3.

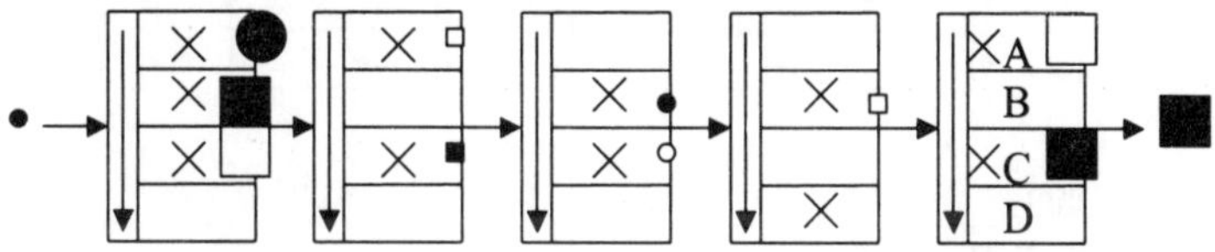

4.

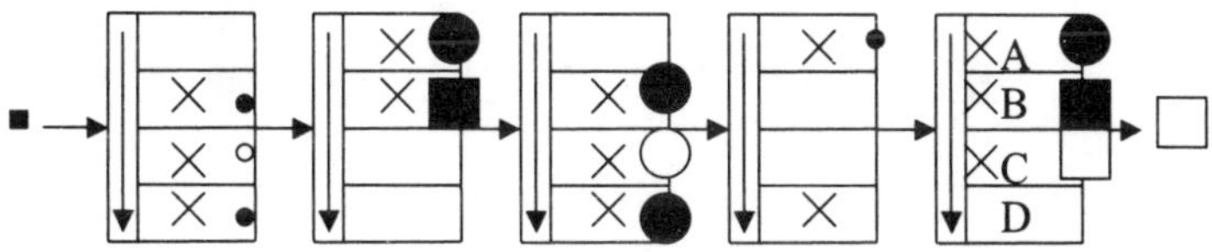

5.

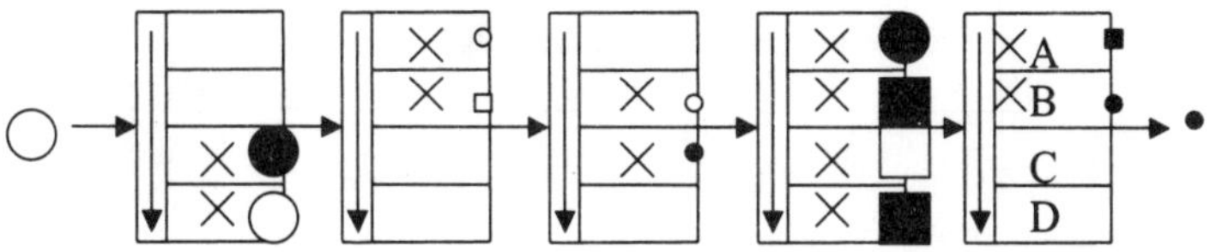

6.

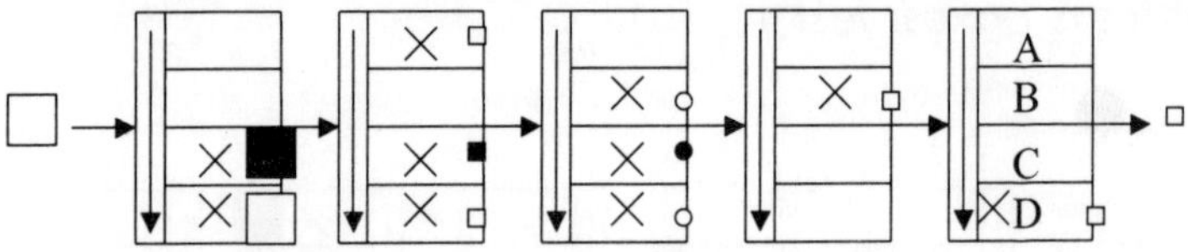

7.

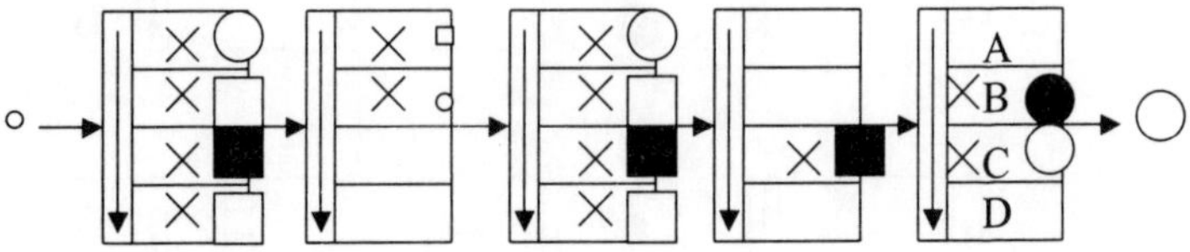

8.

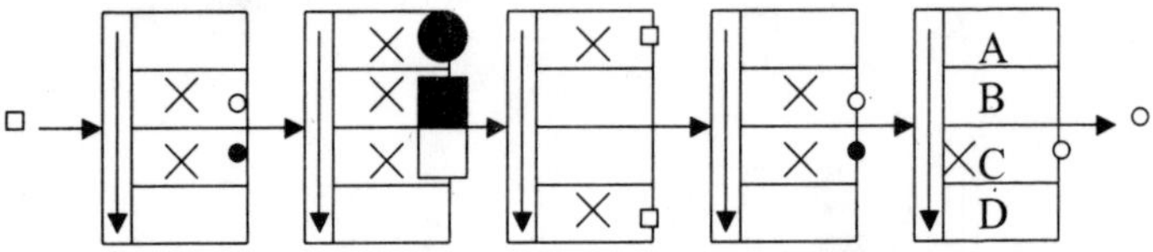

9.

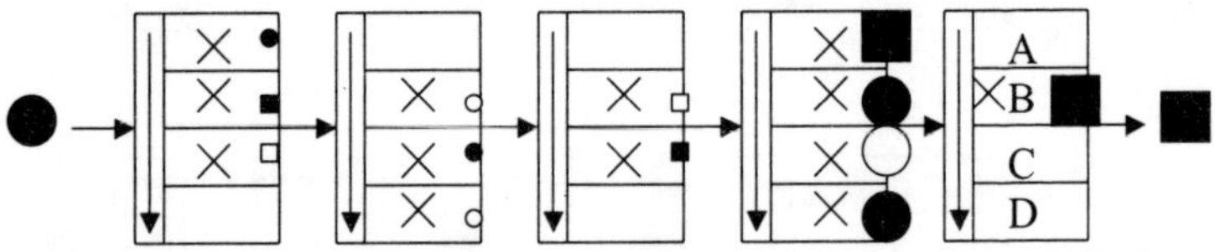

10.

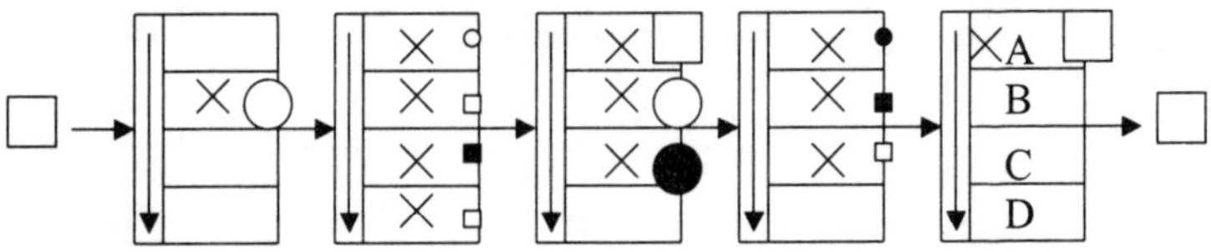

11.

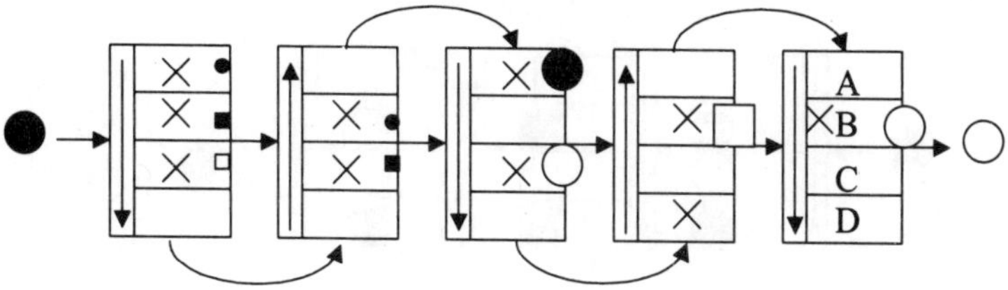

12.

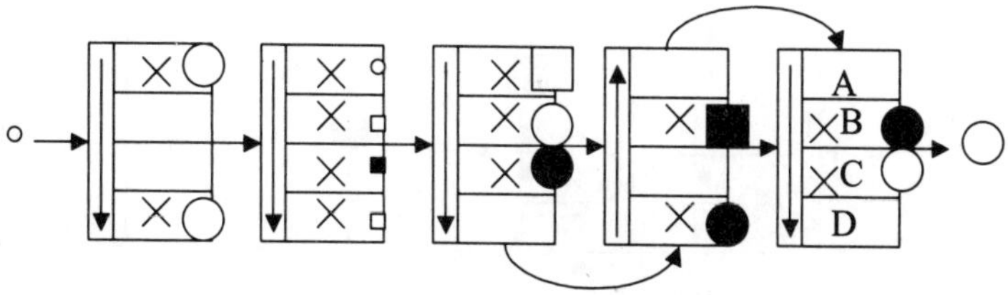

13.

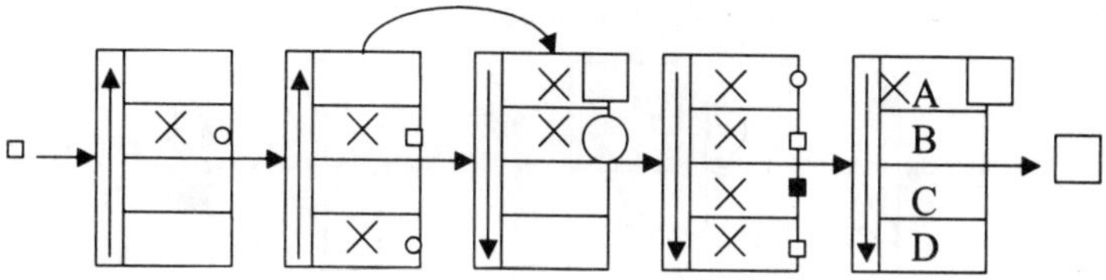

14.

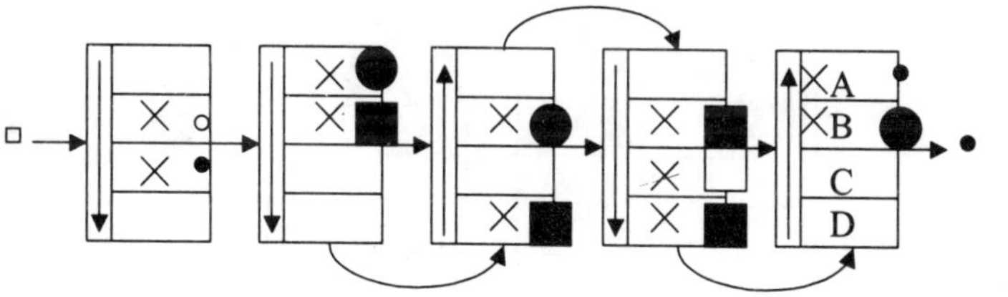

15.

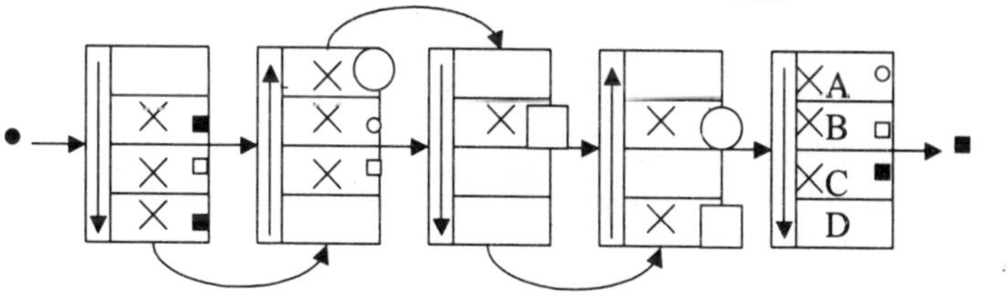

16.

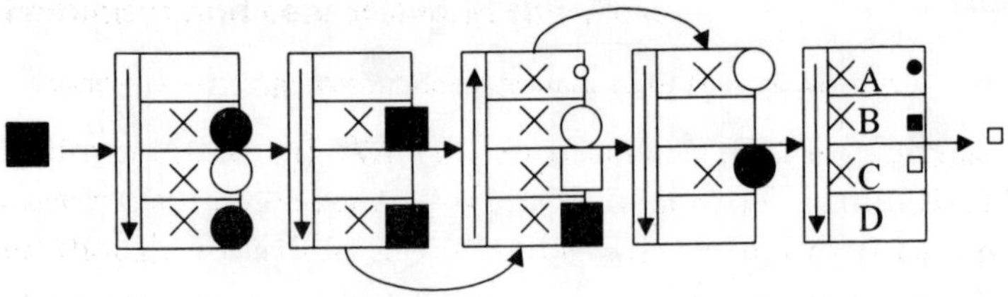

17.

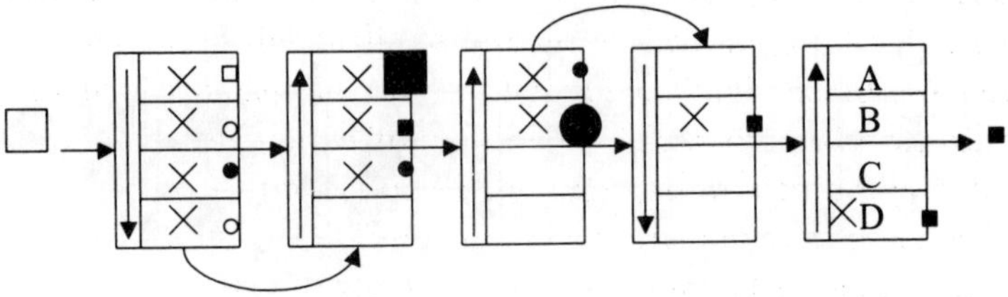

18.

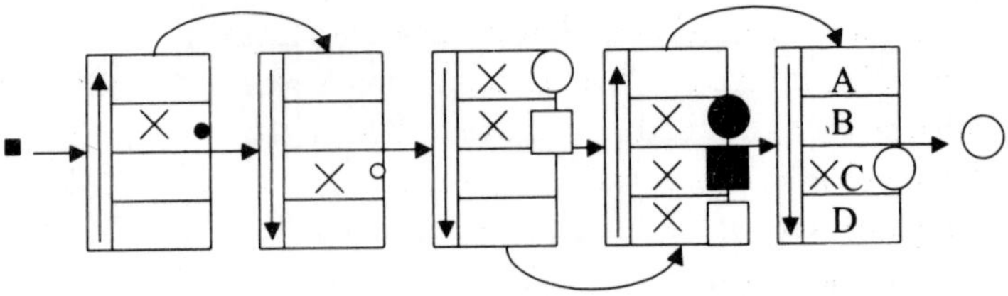

19.

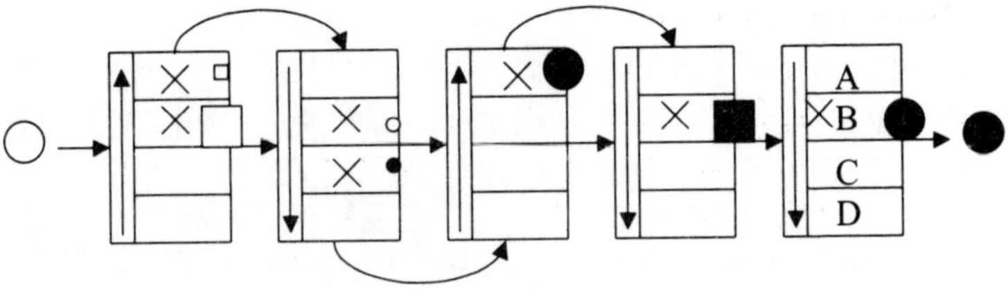

20.

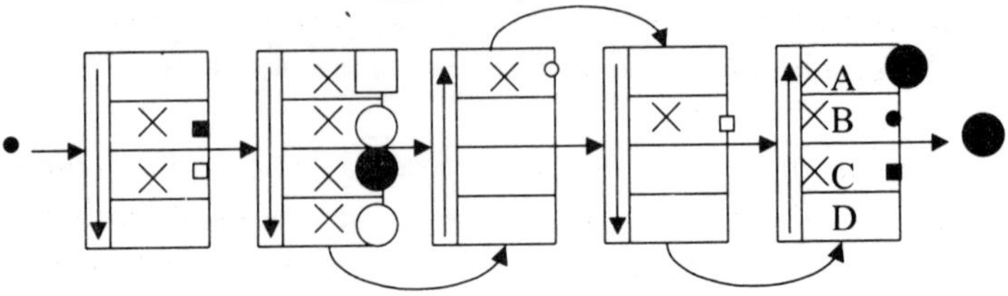

Test 2

1. A
2. B
3. C
4. D
5. A
6. D
7. C
8. B
9. A
10. D
11. A
12. B
13. C
14. D
15. A
16. B
17. C
18. D
19. B
20. D

Solution for diagrammatic reasoning tests using control process boxes: test 2

1.

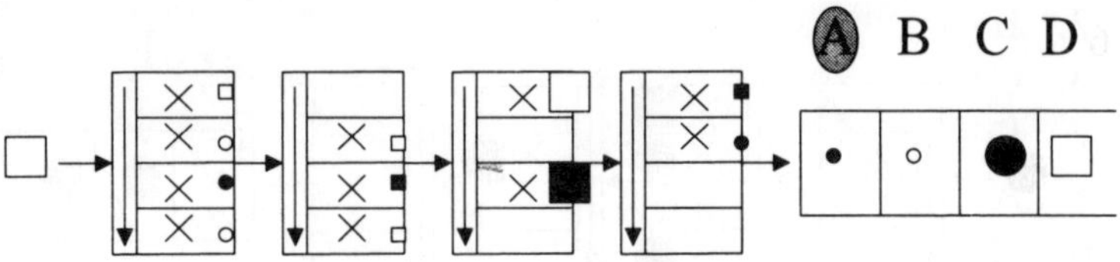

2.

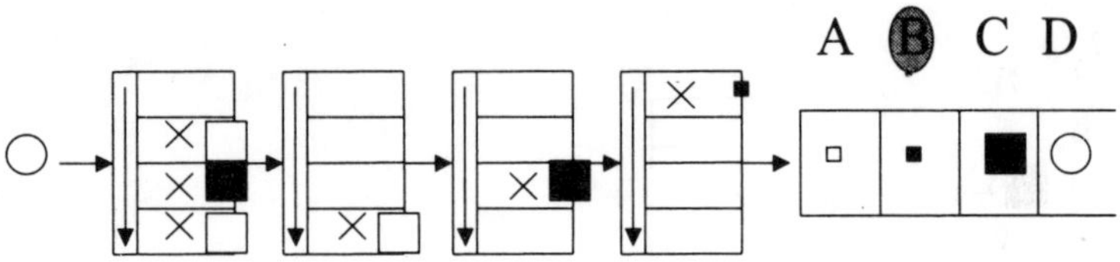

3.

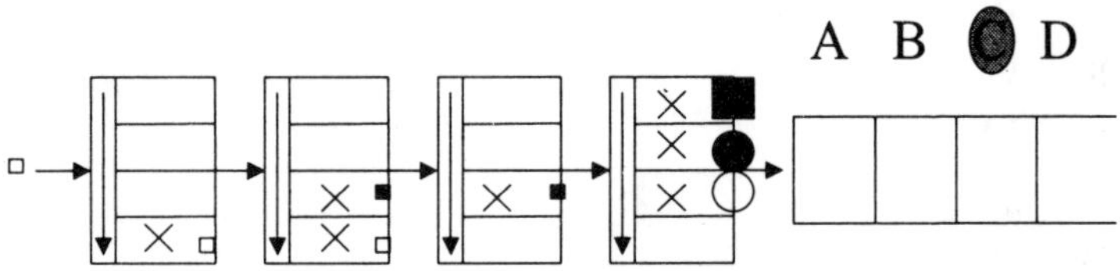

4.

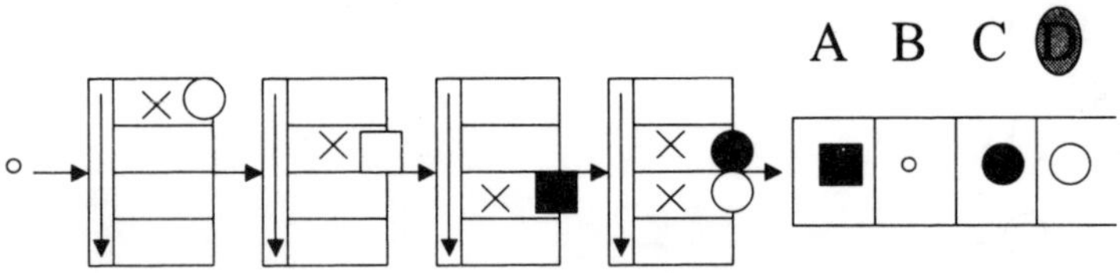

5.

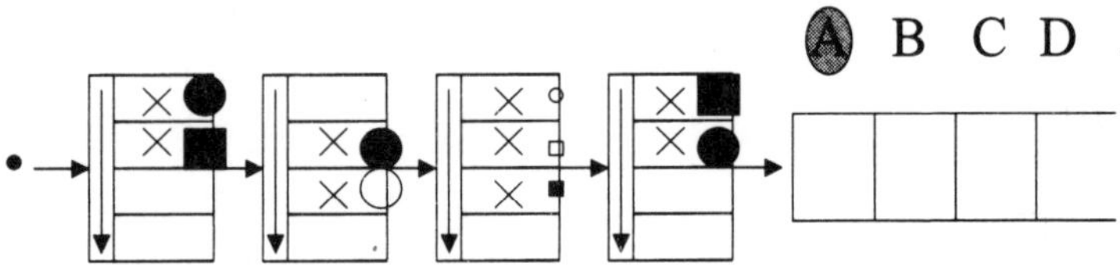

6.

A B C D

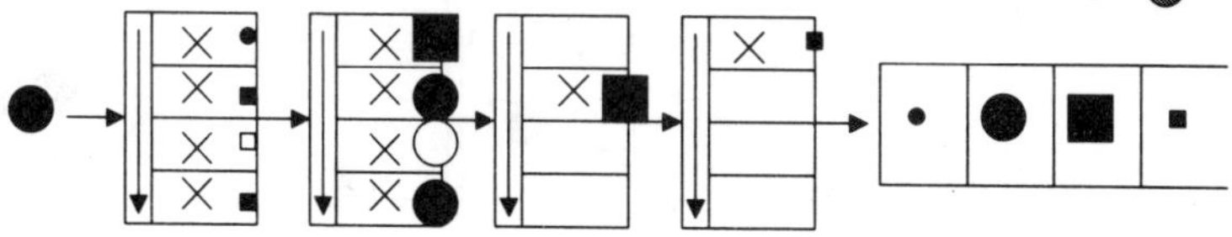

7.

A B C D

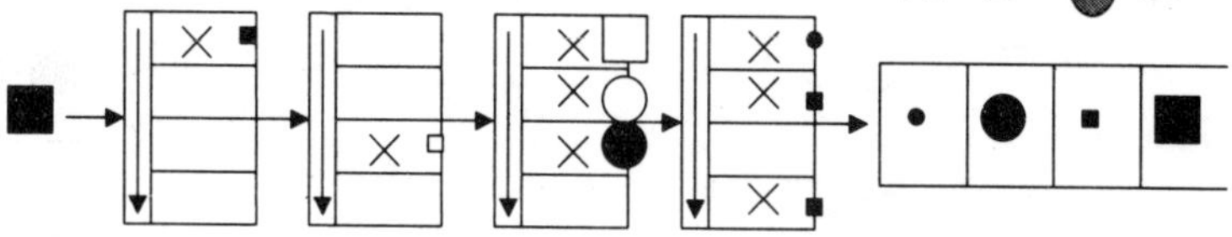

8.

A B C D

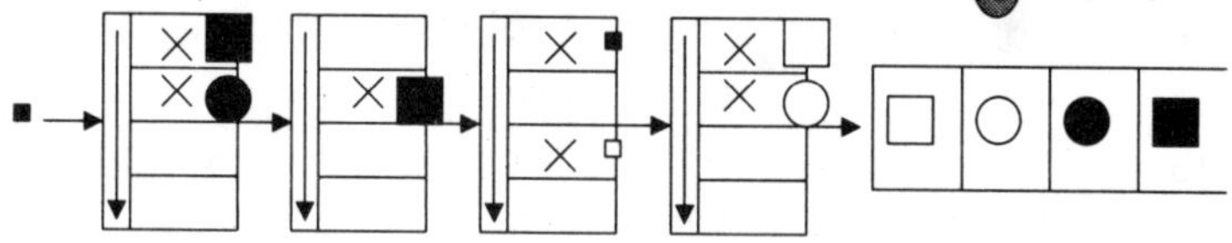

9.

A B C D

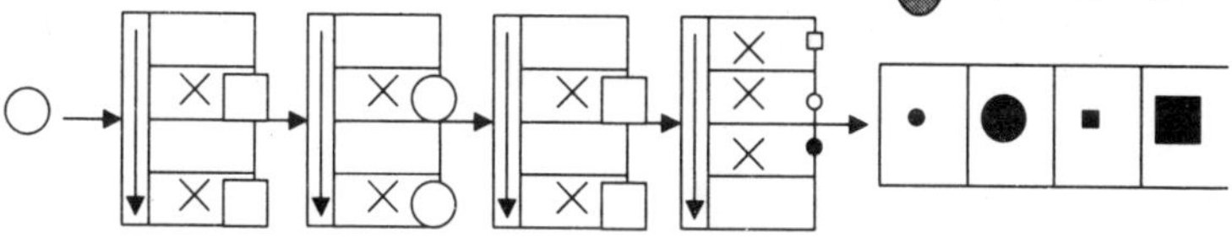

10.

A B C D

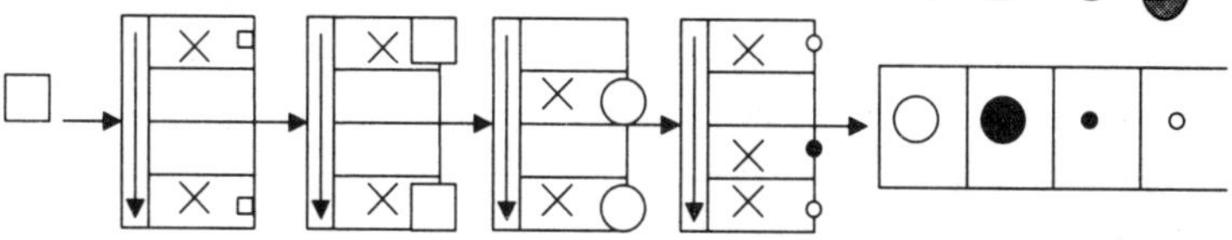

11. **A** B C D

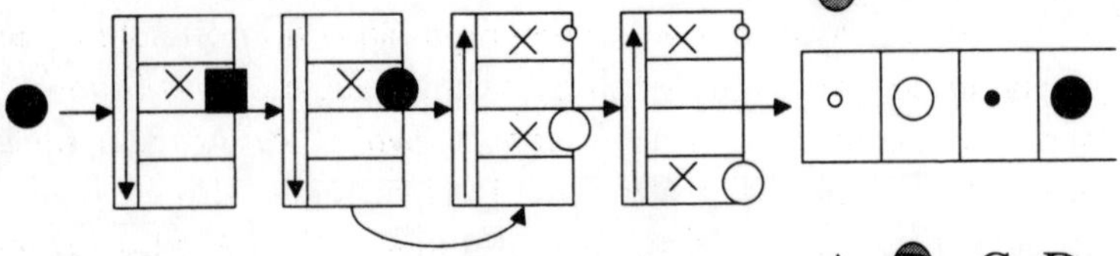

12. A **B** C D

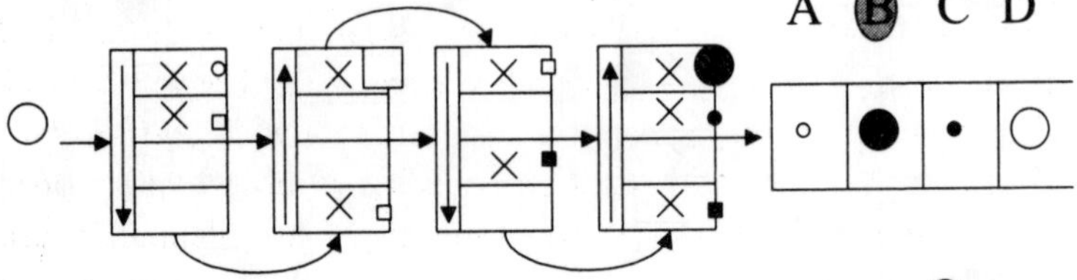

13. A B **C** D

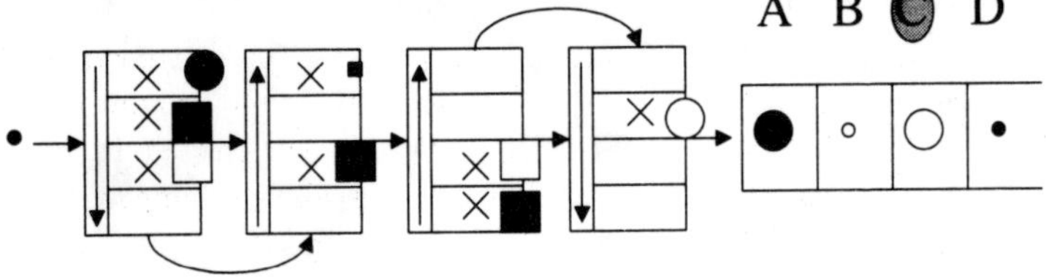

14. A B C **D**

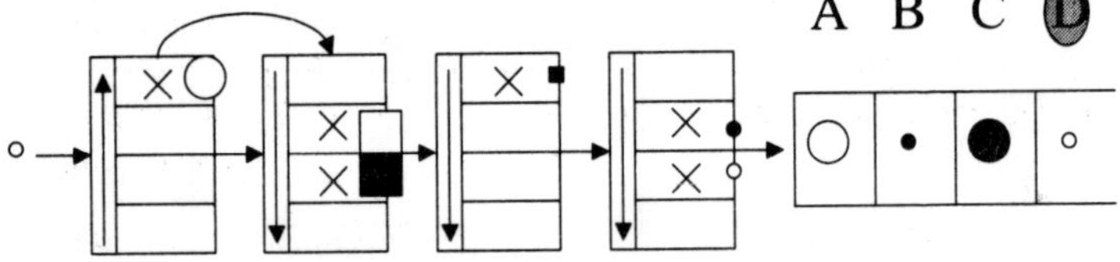

15. **A** B C D

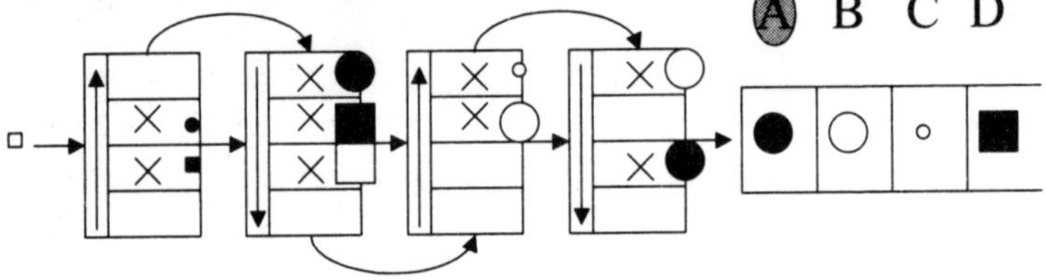

16. A B C D

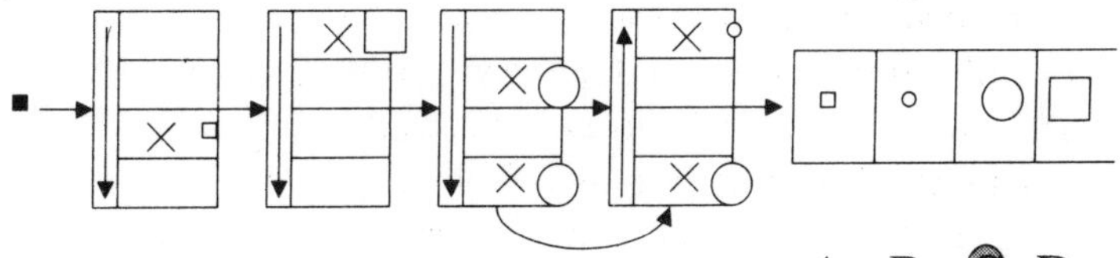

17. A B C D

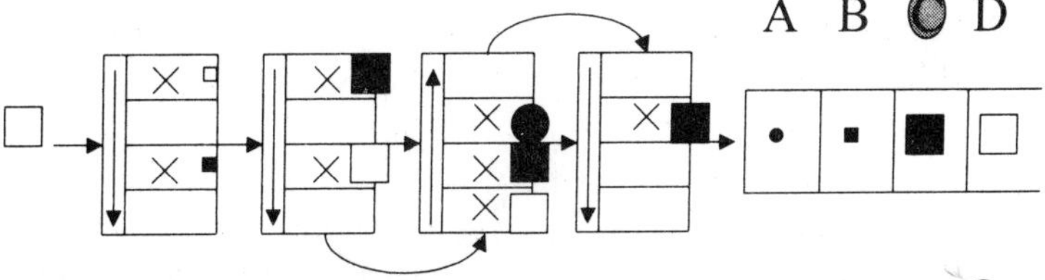

18. A B C D

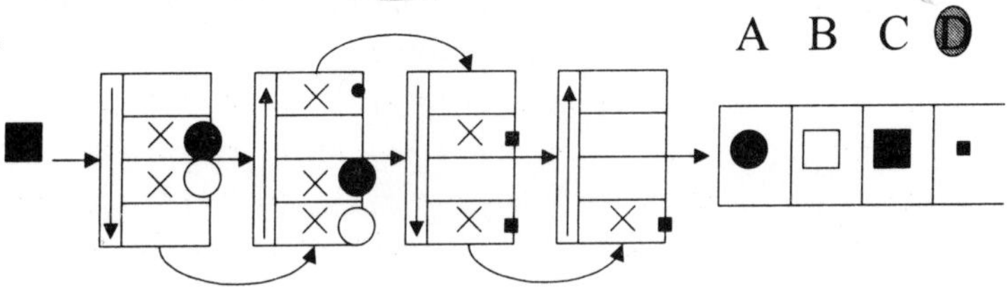

19. A B C D

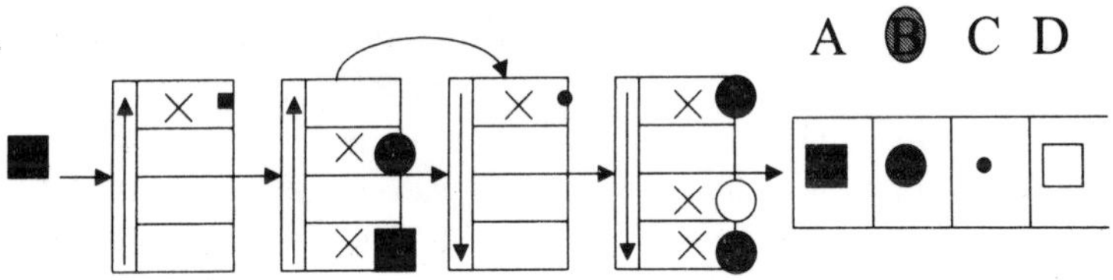

20. A B C D

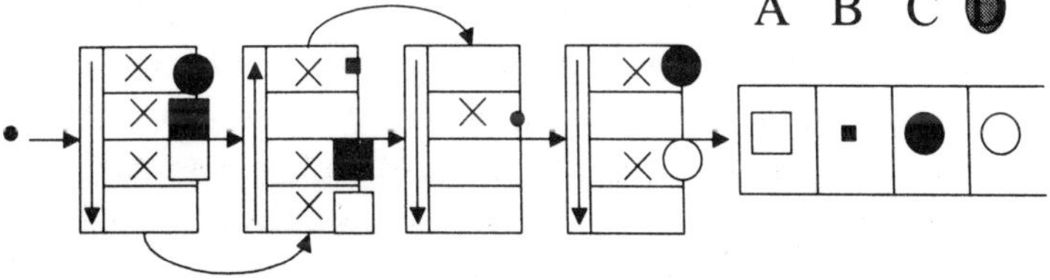

2

Psychometric tests for finance and management

Number series

This type of test is popular and used extensively in recruitment to test basic numerical reasoning abilities. The test consists of a sequence of numbers and your task is to find out the pattern and progression of the sequences, then find the number to replace the question mark (?) in the sequences, by selecting one from four provided choices, as illustrated below:

Example 1

9	18	36	?

A	B	C	D
72	59	63	54

In this sequence each number is increased by multiplying by (2):

9 (×2) = 18 (×2) = 36 (×2) =? = 72, therefore the answer is A.

Example 2

29	2	31	33	?

A	B	C	D
63	64	2	54

In this sequence the two previous numbers are added to obtain the next number in the series. 31 is obtained by adding 29 + 2; 33 is obtained by adding 2 + 31. Therefore ? is equal to 31 + 33 = 64, therefore the answer is B.

Tips

- I have provided in this test most of the common types of series you might expect in your actual test. I suggest you first attempt and take the test within the time limit, then go to the end of the chapter where you will find the answers and learn how the different series of numbers are constructed. After you feel confident that you have understood all the basic principles, try to take the test again and see the differences by comparing your results with first attempt.
- This test deals with basic principles of arithmetic and you have to use quick mental arithmetic to answer the questions; usually, calculators are not allowed in this test. I recommend that you read the tips on numerical estimation tests in Chapter 5 in this book to help you to develop the quick mental arithmetic skills necessary to improve your speed and performance.

Now try the number series test below, which consists of 40 questions, without the use of a calculator, and see how many you can answer in 10 minutes by selecting one of the four choices, ie A, B, C, D. Mark your answer on a sheet of paper and compare your results with the answer provided at the end of this chapter.

No.	Series						A	B	C	D
1.	2	8	14	?	26		19	20	18	21
2.	3	6	?	24	48		12	10	14	16
3.	19	16	?	10	7		11	12	13	14
4.	81	27	9	?	1		4	1	2	3
5.	0.5	1.1	?	2.3	2.9		1.7	1.5	1.4	1.3
6.	1.9	3.8	7.6	?	30.4		15.2	13.2	16.4	14.2
7.	9	10	12	15	19	?	26	22	23	24
8.	?	22	16	11	7	4	33	31	29	28
9.	29	19	48	67	?		88	115	114	108
10.	2	5	10	?	500		60	300	50	100

Question									A	B	C	D
11.	4	?	16	32	64				6	12	10	8
12.	3	3	?	18	72				6	18	9	8
13.	?	36	34	33	33				37	38	39	41
14.	72	?	6	3	3				24	26	54	18
15.	9	4	5	1	2	?			-1	3	1	4
16.	17	18	16	19	15	?			20	17	22	14
17.	37	36	38	35	39	34	?		42	38	36	40
18.	8	16	18	?	38				30	26	24	36
19.	11	13	39	?	123				81	41	61	72
20.	13	10	30	?	81				32	45	27	29

											A	B	C	D
21.	2	6	3	9	13	10	?	34			30	14	29	18
22.	8	24	12	14	42	21	?	69			24	23	43	33
23.	3	12	11	44	43	?					45	47	72	172
24.	6	10	13	11	15	18	16	?			23	21	20	17
25.	2	8	4	16	4	16	8	?	8		16	32	4	24
26.	25	5	25	30	6	30	35	?			8	9	7	32
27.	1	2	4	2	4	6	?				6	3	4	1
28.	16	8	32	16	64	?	128				32	80	96	72
29.	7	12	24	29	?	63					24	34	45	58
30.	1	3	3	18	18	?					90	72	36	162

No.	Series									A	B	C	D
31.	1	1	3	3	7	9	13	?		27	17	19	21
32.	9	1.5	6	3	3	6	1	?		1	6	9	12
33.	1	8	27	64	125	?				96	116	216	210
34.	3	-9	27	-81	?					243	162	180	198
35.	7	9	13	21	37	?				41	47	69	57
36.	67	13	54	87	26	61	23	1	?	22	88	24	42
37.	81	0.5	9	0.75	1	1	?			0.11	1.25	0.75	2
38.	33	32	34	31	35	30	36	29	?	33	37	39	41
39.	69	96	33	11	11	33	?	69		93	66	96	63
40.	79	8	87	95	182	?				277	212	192	276

Character series

Character series is one of the tests commonly used by big organizations instead of number series. Therefore my advice is to be prepared for both in case the organization does not tell you which one they will use. In this test you will be presented with a character series and you are asked to find the correct rules and complete the series. A series can start from any point in the alphabet (A–Z) and you have to work out which sequences to use.

Tips

For many candidates, character series tests offer the opportunity to add extra points to their overall performance during the assessment day. Write the alphabetical series (A–Z) on a separate scrap of paper to help you visualize the order of all the characters and then work out the sequences as quickly and accurately as possible. I personally wrote the sequences about 5 times during the practice session on separate paper, so if I marked one erroneously, I would already have another one available without using a rubber. Look at the examples below.

Example 1

	1	2	3	4	5
X Y X Y X Y X Y	X	Y	Z	V	W

For this example, the series goes: XY XY XY XY
The next letter in the series is X. Choice 1.

Example 2

V V W W X X Y Y	1 U	2 S	3 T	4 Z	5 Q

In example 2, the series goes like this: VV WW XX YY
The next letter in the series is Z. Choice 4.

Now try example 3 below and indicate the correct answer on separate paper.

Example 3

V J W J X J Y J	1 L	2 M	3 Z	4 O	5 P

In example 3, the series goes: VJ WJ XJ YJ

Therefore, the correct answer is Z, choice 3. Finally, do example 4 and indicate the correct answer, which is one of the letters on the right-hand side of the page.

Example 4

a b c d a b c d a b c	1 d	2 a	3 b	4 c	5 e

In example 4, the series goes like this: abcd abcd abc

Therefore, the correct answer is d, choice 1.

When you are ready and confident that you have understood the concept above, try the 36 questions and allow yourself 8 minutes to finish.

Practice questions

															1	2	3	4	5
1.	B	B	C	D	D	E	F	F							C	H	G	K	I
2.	M	S	M	T	N	S	N	T	O						O	T	S	P	M
3.	J	K	L	J	K	L	M	N	O						M	N	O	P	Q
4.	K	L	M	K	L	N	K	L	O						M	N	O	K	P
5.	A	B	L	M	N	A	B	O	P						R	S	M	N	Q
6.	A	B	C	V	A	B	C	W	A	B	C	X			A	B	C	Y	Z
7.	M	N	O	P	Q	O	R	S	O	T	U	O			T	V	W	X	Y
8.	q	p	o	q	p	o	q	p	o	q	p	o			o	p	r	s	q
9.	U	V	V	W	X	X	Y	Z							Z	V	W	X	Y
10.	h	t	u	q	r	s	h	t	u						s	u	t	q	h
11.	a	b	d	e	g	h	j	k							l	m	n	o	p
12.	K	L	M	M	N	O	P	P							Q	R	S	T	U
13.	A	V	W	B	X	Y	C								A	X	Y	Z	V
14.	p	p	r	r	t	t	v	v							x	y	z	v	a
15.	I	I	I	H	H	G	F	F	F	E					G	H	E	F	D

															1	2	3	4	5
16.	C	D	C	D	A	B	E	F	E	F	A	B			K	G	H	I	J
17.	I	J	J	K	K	K	L	L	L						O	K	N	L	M
18.	R	Q	P	O											M	O	P	L	N
19.	J	K	L	S	T	M	N	O	S	T					Q	P	R	S	T
20.	o	q	s	u											v	t	o	w	x
21.	r	s	t	r	s	t	u	r	s	t	u	v			t	s	r	x	w
22.	r	s	r	t	u	t	v	w	v	x	y				y	x	z	w	t
23.	W	W	X	W	X	Y	Y	Z	Y						Y	X	Z	W	V
24.	N	X	O	P	X	Q	R	S	X						S	T	U	V	Q
25.	a	c	f	j											p	o	n	m	r
26.	K	L	N	O	R	S									W	X	V	U	T
27.	m	p	n	q	o	r	p								t	u	v	r	s
28.	o	u	p	v	q										v	p	w	x	y
29.	E	H	L	O	S										W	X	Y	V	Z
30.	C	D	E	F	G	I	J	K	L	N	O	P			R	S	T	U	V
31.	D	G	I	L	N										P	Q	R	S	T
32.	k	p	u	l	q										u	v	w	t	x
33.	u	a	r	d	o										f	h	g	k	l
34.	A	L	M	B	P	Q	C								R	S	U	T	V
35.	A	B	X	C	D	Y	E	F							Y	W	H	G	Z
36.	Q	W	P	X	O	Y	N								Z	X	R	S	T

Quantitative relations tests

Usually in this test you are given a table of 3 rows and 3 columns. In each row there is a numerical relationship, which is the same for all the rows in the same table. Your task is to work out this numerical relationship and to replace the question mark in one of the rows with an appropriate number, using the other two rows as your guide. You do this by choosing one of the four answers provided, as illustrated in the example below:

X	Y	Z
19	7	24
33	15	36
12.8	5.3	?

A	B	C	D
12	15	16	17

The relationship within each row is:

X – Y = Z/2
First row: 19 – 7 = **24**/2 = 12
Second row: 33 – 15 = **36**/2 = 18
Third row: 12.8 – 5.3 = **15**/2 = 7.5

Therefore you should select B = 15 as your answer to replace the question mark.

Tips

- Might I suggest that you first attempt to take this test within the given time limit, then go to the end of the chapter; where you will find the answers. Scrutinize all the numerical relationships thoroughly for every question and understand how they are formed. If you feel confident that you have understood all the different numerical relationship possibilities, then try to take the test again; compare your result with the first attempt and see the difference.

- This test deals with basic principles of numerical relationship; therefore the ability to use quick mental arithmetic could save you valuable time during the actual test. Again, I recommend that you read the tips on numerical estimation tests in Chapter 5 in this book to help you to develop quick mental arithmetic skills.

Now try the test opposite, which consists of 32 questions that must be answered within a time limit of 16 minutes.

1.

X	Y	Z
69	15	54
30	?	28
13	2	11

A	B	C	D
2	3	4	6

2.

X	Y	Z
84	9	?
72	37	218
60	15	150

A	B	C	D
106	166	176	186

3.

X	Y	Z
?	4	6
35	19	8
92	38	27

A	B	C	D
20	16	12	14

4.

X	Y	Z
12	9	?
11	33	66
8	3	27

A	B	C	D
35	40	45	55

5.

X	Y	Z
27	16	43
18	70	88
66	?	96

A	B	C	D
25	40	35	30

6.

X	Y	Z
4	9	45
5	11	66
5	?	18

A	B	C	D
2	4	3	9

7.

X	Y	Z
55	5	12
84	12	?
46	2	24

A	B	C	D
6	8	12	16

8.

X	Y	Z
80	32	1280
14	12	?
41	4	82

A	B	C	D
84	74	94	14

9.

X	Y	Z
15	12	181
8	33	265
?	29	204

A	B	C	D
7	9	13	11

10.

X	Y	Z
?	5	47
19	2	35
8	12	93

A	B	C	D
12	10	42	7

11.

X	Y	Z
20	?	30
15	3	16
42	18	58

A	B	C	D
22	40	12	10

12.

X	Y	Z
5	28	19
1	?	10
3	92	49

A	B	C	D
32	22	16	18

13.

X	Y	Z
1	6	10
9	70	82
?	0	27

A	B	C	D
19	29	24	27

14.

X	Y	Z
3	80	23
2	28	9
57	?	77

A	B	C	D
90	80	70	60

15.

X	Y	Z
2	14	?
1	10	6
15	30	30

A	B	C	D
9	5	11	13

16.

X	Y	Z
?	10	28
6	15	36
3	3	9

A	B	C	D
12	18	9	8

17.

X	Y	Z
27	15	12
25	?	19
92	12	80

A	B	C	D
8	17	13	6

18.

X	Y	Z
42	5	9
30	2	8
?	1	4

A	B	C	D
15	20	10	25

19.

X	Y	Z
?	8	7
88	11	19
73	13	12

A	B	C	D
43	41	33	31

20.

X	Y	Z
42	81	3
20	29	?
15	11	19

A	B	C	D
9	11	17	23

21.

X	Y	Z
15	2	3
10	?	17
22	4	14

A	B	C	D
7	5	3	9

22.

X	Y	Z
21	3	6
63	9	?
81	27	18

A	B	C	D
27	8	21	18

23.

X	Y	Z
11	8	80
10	7	63
?	13	13

A	B	C	D
1	2	4	6

24.

X	Y	Z
3.5	1.2	2.3
9.6	?	7.4
33.8	12.5	21.3

A	B	C	D
4.2	2.4	3.3	2.2

25.

X	Y	Z
6.4	0.9	6.5
6.8	1.6	6.2
?	7.2	8

A	B	C	D
14.2	16.4	18.6	15

26.

X	Y	Z
11	13.1	?
40	2.5	22.5
19	3.4	12.9

A	B	C	D
20.4	18.6	11.6	16.8

27.

X	Y	Z
2.3	6.9	2.3
2.5	18.5	?
7.4	23.2	7.9

A	B	C	D
8.2	8	7.8	6.9

28.

X	Y	Z
3.3	9.9	11.6
1.2	2.8	6.6
1.4	?	11

A	B	C	D
5.8	6.4	7.4	8.6

29.

X	Y	Z
?	9.9	3.3
5	21.2	5.3
9	32.8	4.1

A	B	C	D
7	8.4	6.2	4

30.

X	Y	Z
2	26.4	6.6
6	13.6	1.7
?	10.8	2.7

A	B	C	D
6.1	5.3	4	2

31.

X	Y	Z
6.7	21	17.3
3.4	37	36.6
8.4	17	?

A	B	C	D
11.6	12.3	9.6	6.11

32.

X	Y	Z
89.9	10.9	70
75.4	14.4	?
13.2	2.5	1.7

A	B	C	D
50	52	49.3	41.4

Logical pattern and sequences

This is the ability to think strictly logically in abstract terms. In this test you are given a row of four figures on the left-hand side of the page and four figures on the right-hand side of the page. The four figures on the left-hand side contain several symbols, patterned in a logical sequence, and you are asked to discover how the sequence is constructed and how it works. When you have found that, then you have to complete the logical sequence with one and only one figure from the right-hand side of the page on the same row. Look at the examples below.

Example 1

A B C D

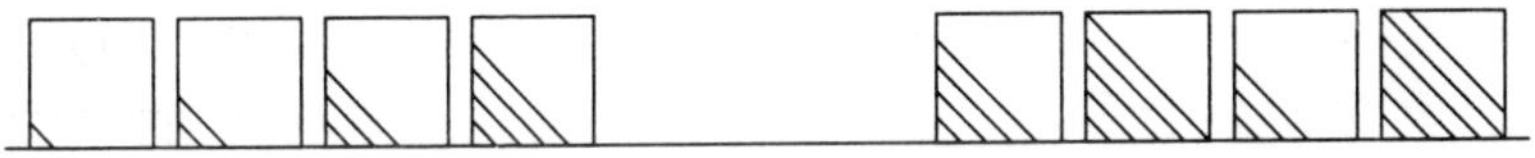

The answer is B, as there have to be 5 lines in the square. (1st square 1 line, 2nd square 2 lines, 3rd square 3 lines, and so on).

Example 2

A B C D

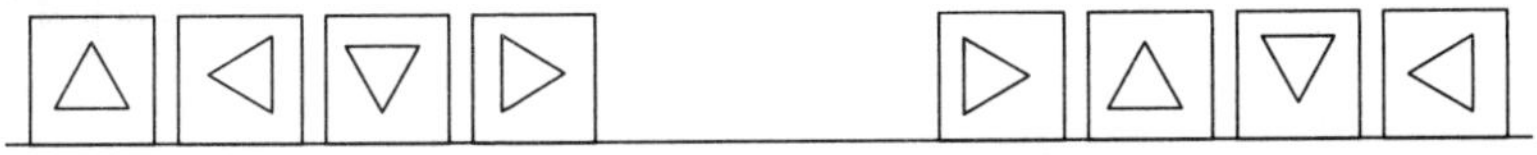

The answer is B, as the triangle movement is 90 degrees anti-clockwise. The next or fifth position would thus be pointing upward.

Example 3

A B C D

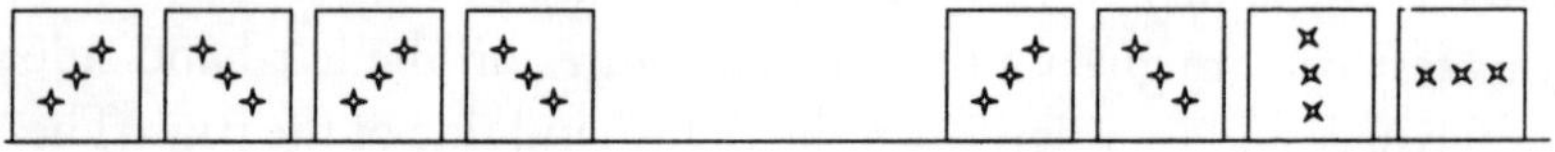

The answer is A. The stars form alternate diagonals.

When you are ready and confident that you have understood the concept above, try the 25 questions and allow yourself 5 minutes to finish.

A B C D

1. 

2. 

3. 

4. 

5. 

6. 

7. 

A B C D

8. 

9. 

10. 

11. 

12. 

13. 

14. 

15. 

16. 

17. 

18. 

A B C D

19. 

20. 

21. 

22. 

23. 

24. 

25. 

Table checking

Usually very little time is allowed in tests of this kind; 8–15 seconds per question, depending on the test and the company providing the test. Therefore, it is important to work quickly and accurately. Depending on which company is providing the test, there are many ways the test is presented. What is given here is a flavour of what you may get in your actual test, and I leave it to your creativity to design further examples and set the time limit to meet your ability. However, I will mention here, briefly, a few examples from the popular formats. The test could be presented in the form of an original column with items, ie a string of characters, symbols, etc, to compare with a typed copy which differs from the original organized in single columns; you have to pinpoint the differences.

Example 1 Single column

Original	Typed copy
A B C D 5 E 6 F 7 G 8 H 9	A B C D 5 6 F 7 G 8 H 9

As you can see from the above example, the character E is missing in the typed copy.

In another form you would have to compare the first-column string of letters and numbers with a number of copies in different columns and again mark the mistakes in each column as shown below.

Example 2 Multiple columns

Original	Copy 1	Copy 2	Copy 3
X Y Z % T &	Z % T &	X Y Z &	X Y Z % T &

Copy 4
X Y % T &

As you can see, XY is missing in the second column (copy 1), % and T are missing from the third column (copy 2), there are no mistakes in the copy 3 column and finally Z is missing from the copy 4 column.

Another type involves comparing sets of characters or symbols arranged in pairs, one on the left and another on the right, and pinpointing how many pairs are identical in a single question.

Example 3 Arranged in two pairs

ILOVE	ILOV
SD&M7	SD&M7
ROTOR	ROTOR

In the above example, two of the three given pairs are identical.

Another way is to identify the identical pair from several columns on each row.

Example 4 Identify identical pair from among many columns

A	B	C	D
XYZ232	XYZ332	XYZ234	XYZ232

E
XZY232

For the above example we have only one identical pair in columns A and D. Of course, in all of these examples you will be provided with a separate sheet on which to mark your answers.

Tips

Valid only for example 4 models – as I took the test below myself and saw the benefits. My advice is to take four or five letters or numbers (depending on your ability) from the beginning or end of column A and compare with the rest. When you find the matches, compare the remaining character(s). The choice of four letters is optional and could be from any column. See the diagram below.

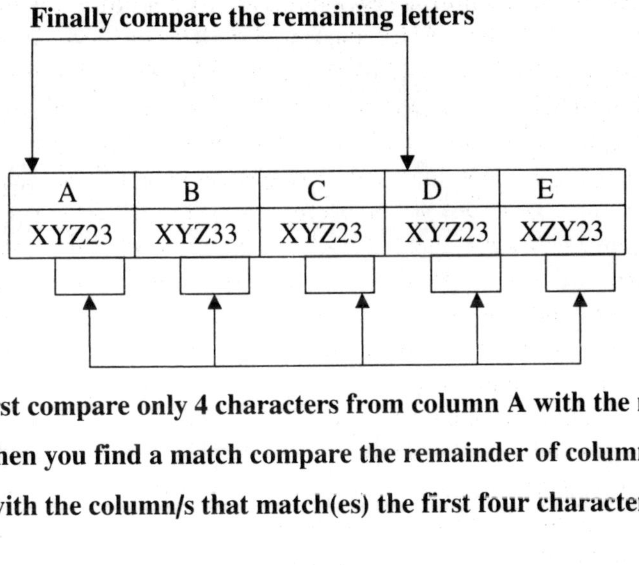

First compare only 4 characters from column A with the rest

When you find a match compare the remainder of column A with the column/s that match(es) the first four characters

When you are ready and confident that you have understood the concept above, try the test below and allow yourself 7 minutes to finish. Mark the two identical sets of letters or numbers of the appropriate columns (A, B, C, D, E or F) on a separate answer sheet.

	A	B	C	D	E	F
i.	XNM23%	XNL23%	MXN23%	NXM23%	XNM32%	XNM23%
ii.	1*$2RTY	12*$RTY	1*2$RTY	1*2$RYT	1*2$RTY	1*2R$TY
iii.	OPQ65K	OPQ56K	OQP56K	OPQ56K	QOP56K	KOPQ56
iv.	XCVBN	XCVBN	XCBVN	XCVNB	XVCBN	XCBNV
v.	LNM$*W	LNM*$W	MN*$WL	LMN*$W	LMN$*W	LMN*$W
vi.	GHI49!	HGI4=9!	GHI4=9!	GHI4=!9	GHI4=9!	GHI=49!
vii.	TRE&R%	TRER&%	TER&R%	TRE %	TRE&R%	TR&ER%
viii.	DCE?R*	CDE?R*	CDE?R*	CDE? *R	CED?R*	CDER*?
ix.	TIR6532	IRT6532	ITR5632	ITR6523	ITR6532	ITR6532
x.	JQ&W80$	JQW&80$	JQW&08$	JQW&80$	JQW&8$0	QJW&80$
xi.	A*D65&	A*D6&5	A*D65&	A*D56&	A D *65&	A*65 D &
xii.	#4T&(R*	#4T&R(*	#4TR& (*	4#&R(*	#4T&R(*	4#T& (*
xiii.	8Q5TH?	QT85H?	Q85T?H	Q85TH?	Q58TH?	Q85TH?
xiv.	2 M ^$5K	M2^$ K 5	M2^5$K	M2^$5K	M2^$5K	M^2$5K
xv.	0LO4K%	0LKO4%	0LKO4%	0LOK4%	0LK4O%	L0KO4%
xvi.	VW8$42	WV48$2	VW4$82	VW48$2	VW48$2	WV482$
xvii.	TRL9#%	TRL9%#	TRL9#%	RTL9#%	TR9#L%	TR9L%#
xviii.	KL4&#W	KL4#&W	K4L&#W	KL4&#W	KWL4&#	L4K&#W
xix.	POI7834	PIO7834	PO7I834	POI7483	POI7384	POI7834
xx.	?3ERNV	?83ERVN	?83ENRV	?8E3RNV	?83ERVN	?8ERNV
xxi.	FLE9@4	LEF9@4	LFE9@4	LF9E@4	LFE94@	LFE9@4
xxii.	OTR731	OTR71	OT731	OR731	OTR731	ORT71
xxiii.	OP?\24%	PO?\24%	OP\?24%	OP?2\4%	OP?\24	OP?\24%
xxiv.	XC8*L?3	X8*L?3	X8C*L?3	XC8L*?3	XC8*L3?	XC8*L?3
xxv.	MN$L9%	MN$%L9	MN%L9	ML N%$9	NM$%9	MN$%L9
xxvi.	56P78H$	56P78$H	56P87H$	5P678H$	56P78H$	65P78H$
xxvii.	%M&7*T	%M7&*T	M7% &*T	%M7*T&	%M7&*T	%M7&T *
xxviii.	#OYT%	#YT*%	#OYT*%	#OYT*%	#OT*%	OYT*%
xxix.	PTR68!	PR68!	TPR68!	PTR86!	PTR68!	TRP68!
xxx.	TR6&231	TR6&321	TR63&21	TR6&321	TR&621	TR6&31
xxxi.	E4R5T6G	4ER5T6G	E4R56GT	E4RT56G	E4R5T6G	EG4R5T6
xxxii.	O15REW	OT4REW	0T5RWE	OT5REW	OT5REW	OT5RFW
xxxiii.	IT&D*$	IT&D*$	IT&D$*	T1&D*$	IT&D$	ITD*$
xxxiv.	LKD579	L5KD97	LK5D97	LDK597	LKD597	LKD597
xxxv.	QSA&$T	QAS&$T	QAS&$T	QAS&T$	QAS$T	QA&$T
xxxvi.	9RT67	69RT67	69R67	6RT67	69RT67	6RT76
xxxvii.	JDSETI4	JDSTI4	JSETI4	JDSET4	JDSETI	JDSETI4
xxxviii.	M56&$	N56$	NM56$&	NM6&$	NM56&$	NM56&$
xxxix.	JTRLNOP	JTLNOP	JTRLNOP	JRLNOP	TRLNOP	JTRLNP
xl.	139587&	1-39587&	1-3587&	1-3957&	1-3958&	1-39587&
xli.	985HTR4	985TR4	985HTR4	85HTR4	95HTR4	985T4R
xlii.	TR24&*	TR47&*	T247&*	TR247&*	TR247&*	TR247&
xliii.	QR%8H	Q%#8H	QR%#8H	QR%#8H	QR#8H	QR%#8

Answers to practice exercises

Number series

1. B +6
2. A × 2
3. C –3
4. D ÷3
5. A +0.6
6. A ×2
7. D +1, +2, +3, +4, +5
8. C –7, –6, –5, –4, –3
9. B Add two previous numbers: 29 + 19 = 48, 48 + 67 = 115
10. C Multiply two previous numbers: 2 × 5 = 10, 5 × 10 = 50
11. D Power of 2: 2^2, 2^3, 2^4, 2^5, 2^6
12. A ×1, ×2, ×3, ×4
13. C –3, –2, –1, 0
14. D ÷4, ÷3, ÷2, ÷1
15. A –5 + 1, –4 + 1, –3 + 1
16. A +1, –2, +3, –4, +5
17. D –1, +2, –3, +4, –5, +6
18. D ×2, +2, ×2, +2
19. B +2, ×3, +2, ×3
20. C –3, ×3, –3, ×3
21. A +4 –3 ×3, +4 –3 ×3, +4 –3 ×3
22. B ×3 ÷2 +2, ×3 ÷2 +2
23. D ×4 –1, ×4 –1, ×4 –1
24. C +4 +3 –2, +4 +3 –2, +4 +3 –2
25. B ×4 ÷2, ×4 ÷4, ×4÷2, ×4÷4
26. C ÷5 ×5 +5, ÷5 ×5 +5
27. B ×2 +2 ÷ 2, ×2 +2 ÷ 2

28. A ÷2 ×4, ÷2 ×4, ÷2 ×4
29. D +5 ×2, +5 ×2, +5 ×2
30. D ×3, ×1, ×6, ×1, ×9, ×1
31. A Hope series: 1st series (1, 3, 7, 13), 2nd series (1, 3, 9, 27)
32. D Hope series: 1st series (9, 6, 3, 1), 2nd series (1.5, 3, 6, 12)
33. C The cubes cubed numbers: 1^3, 2^3, 3^3, 4^3, 5^3
34. A Alternative sign ×3
35. C ×2 –5, ×2 –5, ×2 –5
36. A Subtract two previous numbers: 67 – 13 = 54, 87 – 26 = 61
37. A Hope series:1st series (81, 9, 1, 0.11), 2nd series (0.5, 0.75,1)
38. B –1 +2, –3 +4, –5 +6, –7 +8
39. C Mirror pattern
40. A Add two previous numbers: 79 + 8 = 87, 87 + 95 = 182

Character series

1. 3
2. 3
3. 1
4. 4
5. 5
6. 1
7. 2
8. 5
9. 1
10. 4
11. 2
12. 1
13. 4
14. 1
15. 3
16. 2
17. 4
18. 5
19. 2
20. 4
21. 3
22. 2
23. 3
24. 2
25. 2
26. 1
27. 5
28. 3
29. 4
30. 1
31. 2
32. 2

33. 3
34. 4
35. 5
36. 1

Quantitative relations tests

1. A $X - Y = Z$
2. D $X + Y = Z/2$
3. B $X - Y = 2Z$
4. C $Z - Y = 3X$
5. D $X + Y = Z$
6. C $Z/Y = X + 1$
7. B $X/Y = Z - 1$
8. A $X \times Y = 2Z$
9. A $X \times Y = Z - 1$
10. B $X \times Y = Z + 3$
11. C $Z - Y = X - 2$
12. D $Z - X = Y/2$
13. C $Z - X = Y + 3$
14. B $Z - X = Y/4$
15. A $Z - X = Y/2$
16. D $Z - X = Y \times 2$
17. D $Z + Y = X$
18. A $Z + Y = X/3$
19. A $Z + Y = (X + 2)/3$
20. B $Z + Y = 2X$
21. C $Z + X = Y \times 9$
22. D $X - Y = 3Z$
23. B $Z/Y = X - 1$
24. D $X - Y = Z$
25. A $X - Y = Z - 1$
26. B $Z - Y = X/2$
27. B $Y - X = 2Z$
28. C $Y - X = Z - 5$
29. D $Y/Z = X - 1$
30. D $Y/Z = X + 2$
31. A $X + Z = Y + 3$
32. B $X - Y = Z + 9$

Logical pattern and sequences

1. B
2. C
3. A
4. D
5. A
6. B
7. C
8. D
9. A
10. C
11. A
12. B
13. C
14. D
15. B
16. C
17. B
18. A
19. B
20. C
21. D
22. C
23. B
24. A
25. B

Table checking

1. A&F
2. C&E
3. B&D
4. A&B
5. D&F
6. C&E
7. A&E
8. B&C
9. E&F
10. B&D
11. A&C
12. B&E
13. D&F
14. D&E
15. B&C
16. D&E
17. A&C
18. A&D
19. A&F
20. B&E
21. C&F
22. A&E
23. A&F
24. A&F
25. B&F
26. A&E
27. B&E
28. C&D
29. A&E
30. B&D
31. A&E
32. D&E

33. A&B
34. E&F
35. B&C
36. B&E
37. A&F
38. E&F
39. A&C
40. B&F
41. A&C
42. D&E
43. C&D

3

Psychometric tests for IT

High-level programming language test

Owing to the shortage of well-qualified IT specialists, most companies nowadays recruit people from all walks of life. It is not necessary to have know-how or qualifications in IT subjects; only the desire and ability to think logically is required. Most IT industries offer intensive courses in different high-level programming languages, eg JAVA, C, etc, and it is a matter of time before you become an expert programmer.

High-level languages are geared towards the people writing the program rather than the computer. These languages provide the interface between the user and the machine. They are as close to English as you can get and easy to program since their operations closely resemble the language in which the problem is formulated, rather than the internal computer architecture. However, they are sufficiently scrupulous to allow the computer to translate the program written in the high-level language into machine language. The translation of a program written in high-level language into machine language is accomplished by means of a special computer program called a compiler. Since each computer system has its own machine language, a different compiler is required for each different high-level language. The compiler checks your program for errors.

If there are errors the compiler issues an error message or warning. The compiler checks for a variety of errors, some of which are used here as practice exercises in this test. It is not unusual to have to compile your program many times until all errors have been deleted from the program.

In this book I present two kind of compiler checking. For this exercise you will play the role of the compiler to identify the errors in the mock-up programs described below. If you already have some programming skills, be careful not to confuse yourself, because the programs here don't abide by the usual programming rules used in high-level language. Also, be aware that you will have NO time to compile your program more than once, owing to the tight time set for the test. Therefore, you need to pinpoint errors first time and to work quickly and accurately.

Compiler checking by tracking error

In this test you will find a mock-up of unstructured programming lines taken from a C look-alike language, which contain many errors. The errors have been identified and categorized into three types: syntax error (SE), logical error (LE) and other error (OE). Each of the three types of error has its own set of rules. Using these rules, your task is to trace and determine the exact location of an error in each programming line and then identify what type of error it is, ie SE, LE or OE. If no rule has been broken, cross the column No Error (NE).

Look at the following example:

		SE	LE	OE	NE
1.	Printf ("\n Maximum and minimum of the 3 numbers				

Now look at the following set of rules:

SE rules:	**LE** rules:	**OE** rules:
A – Lines must end in a colon (:).	**A** – Division by zero is not allowed	**A** Lines must begin with semi-colon (;)
B – Number must be between stars, eg *7*.	**B** – All arithmetical expressions must be written in Uppercase. Eg X=Y+7; X1/Y1	**B** Double quotation (") can only be used with Printf statement
C – All characters may be used except @, $.		**C** – Rule A from SE and OE does not apply on the opening brace {.

As you can see, rules A and B in SE have been broken; the line should end in a colon and the number, ie 3, should be between stars. No rules are broken in LE. Rule A has been broken in OE, because of the missing semi-colon at the beginning of the line. Therefore, you should cross the SE and OE columns, as shown below.

		SE	LE	OE	NE
1.	Printf ("\n Maximum and minimum of the 3 numbers	×		×	

Now, try the following exercise. See how many you can complete in 10 minutes, then compare your results with the answers given at the end of this chapter.

		SE	LE	OE	NE
1.	;Include<stdio.h>,				
2.	;Include <math.h>:				
3.	#define (NST):				
4.	;double a1b1/x1, Y3				
5.	;main (11Maxim@),				
6.	;{				
7.	;Printf("na="); X/*0*=Y:				
8.	;Scanf(7)%1f, &a):				
9.	,Printf ("%f,*10*);X				
10.	,(* Calculate ymax @ Ymax, "9"):				
11.	XM=0.5+X2(Y1-Y2):				
12.	;MAX=OR+T:				
13.	;Printf("\n X=8%, Y=8%8+61),				
14.	}				
15.	;Void =X1/Y1+7				
16.	{:				
17.	;X1=A+0.5(B-A(NST):				
18.	;Y1=x(R1):				
19.	If (y1=y2) Then Y1=8+x				
20.	Printf("n Interest Rate");				
21.	:For (c=1; c <=20/0;++ c);				
22.	;L=0.01+n,				
23.	,Return:				
24.	,Scanf("a, @/B):				
25.	;Maximum (x,y):				
26.	;While (N/*0*=X+Y) Then X=Y:				
27.	For (count=1; count<=n; count=1+n)				
28.	,Func1(int n):				
29.	;int y=X:				
30.	;X/0=Y:				
31.	;Return:				
32.	}				
33.	,Int Funct1 (inta1):				
34.	;(int funct2 (X+Y=2)):				
35.	,B=F($):				
36.	,Return;				
37.	;/initialize and read in a value for /:				
38.	; While x=y calculate the average :				
39.	; AVERAGE=X+T-Y:				
40.	;Read in the number:				
41.	;For "(c=x; c<=n c=n+x)":				

Compiler checking by line rules

In this test you are presented with a mock-up programming language, designed to be similar to Pascal. Here, however, the conditions are set for each individual line, rather than for the whole program, as in the previous example. Your task is to discover which conditions, if any, have been broken. If more than one condition is broken, then you mark more than one column. If no conditions are broken, then mark column Z.

Look at the example below:

		W	X	Y	Z
A	Procedure Admittance (X=7:Real; VAR G, B:Real)				

Now look at the following set of rules:

Conditions for line **A** in the program:	Conditions for line **B** in the program:	Conditions for line **C** in the program:
W – Lines must end in a *.	**W** – Lines must begin with the word Return.	**W** – All lines must start with uppercase letter.
X – Number must be between double quotation marks, eg "7".	**X** – All arithmetic expressions must be written in uppercase, eg X = Y + 2.	**X** – Double quotation, ", cannot be used.
Y – All numbers may be used except 5 and 7.	**Y** – All characters may be used except @ and ?.	**Y** – Number must be between brackets, eg (7) + (5).

As you can see, in the example the line is designated by the letter A, so you should look above at the conditions applied to line A. Rules W, X, Y have all been broken as there is no * at the end of the line, the number 7 should be between quotation marks, and number 7 should not have been used. Therefore, you should cross W, X, and Y as shown overleaf:

		W	X	Y	Z
A	Procedure Admittance (X=7:Real; VAR G, B:Real)	×	×	×	

Now, try the following exercise. See how many you can complete in 10 minutes and compare your results with the answers given at the end of this chapter.

			W	X	Y	Z
1.	A	Program A1 A2 A3 *				
2.	B	Return (‘Enter Vol Equal A1, A2, @, 5)				
3.	C	If ABS(9) <0 AND ABS>“3”				
4.	B	Return If no signal output then =X+y				
5.	C	For N=0 to end points Do X=Y				
6.	A	Procedure Traprule (B=7) *				
7.	C	Return SUM=SUMY+X				
8.	B	Retur N=Y+K,				
9.	A	Area=SUMOF+H+“4”+J				
10.	B	Writeln (NI=5-X=?)				
11.	C	Trapezoidal =(2)+“8”---(3)= 4;				
12.	B	Return all procedures to zero if possible?				
13.	C	Var V1, V2, V4 are real,				
14.	A	NO=(10-5)= “7”*				
15.	C	Repeat x[M]=NO +(3)				
16.	B	Array X[K] Until X=Y+1				
17.	A	Function data “6” *				
18.	B	Return To the Upper class				
19.	C	Procedures solution to all x=@+“1”,				
20.	A	Newprogram=“9”---“4”+X=“5”X				
21.	A	For K=I+1 to I---1 Do				
22.	B	Reteren and then H---K=G+I				
23.	C	Writeln Mean = ‘ SUM/N’ - 8;				
24.	A	Read(data) & SUM=X+Y*				
25.	C	m=N*SUM/N (SUM)				
26.	B	Return U=O+5+7				
27.	A	X,Y: Array[1..3]{1..8},				
28.	C	real array “8”+ “3”				
29.	B	Procedure Bestline Return*				
30.	C	Read from (7) To (5)				
31.	A	If Length < “15” then M=N*				
32.	B	If Real AND Imaginary Equal Then X=Y				
33.	C	return(All character+Variables)				
34.	B	While return Y+I=6				
35.	A	Mean=K+T*				
36.	B	Return=X=(9)+K is the total number*				
37.	C	Const A1, 23, “9”, ? and(X)				
38.	A	If length >0 and N<8 then *				
39.	B	While X=10 AND Y=20 Then				
40.	A	Write x>“7” FOR ALL y<X				

Tips

This tip is based on testing a number of my students to see the best way to perform the test quickly and accurately. It has been found that taking all the programming lines in consecutive order is not a good way, because your brain has to keep switching back and forth between the rules for the three error types, ie SE, LE, OE in compiler checking by tracking error, or the different lines A, B or C in compiler checking by line rules. This wastes time and leads to confusion. The best way is to handle one type of error at a time. Take, for example, the previous exercise for compiler checking by line rules. Instead of checking line after line, you simply take the conditions set for line A and test every line in the program where line A is identified, and mark your answer if the conditions are broken. When you have done this, look at the conditions for line B and again go through the whole program and test all lines marked B, and so on. In this way, there are fewer rules to remember, you are less confused and your brain does not have to switch between conditions, so comparison is more accurate and fast. My students improved by about 70 per cent using this approach. However, practice brings mastery.

Assembly language test

Assembly language is a low-level language that is oriented towards the computer rather than the people who are programming the computer. To use a particular assembly language the programmer must have a thorough understanding of the internal architecture of the central processing unit (CPU) of that particular computer. The language consists of a list of instructions made up of mnemonic words and symbols. The number of instructions and commands used depends on the type of CPU, and they can only be executed on computers of identical design. Programming is very time consuming to learn and it takes considerable experience to become proficient. Furthermore, programmers are always occupied with internal details of architecture rather than the actual program task to be accomplished. However, assembly language has a few advantages. First, it runs much faster than high-level language because it is nearer to the fundamental language (machine language, ie writing programs using a series of zeros and ones) for any computer. Second, there are some tasks that require direct access to hardware architecture; these are more easily implemented in assembly language and may be difficult or impossible to do in a high-level language.

Many IT companies are using the basic commands offered by assembly language to develop their own assembly language, which is not related to any particular CPU architecture and is only used for testing candidates' computer aptitudes. Most of the commands and symbols used in these tests are simple if you have previous knowledge of assembly language programming; however, if not, such a test could be a very challenging experience. IT industries claim in their invitation letters that prior programming knowledge is not required; however, it is difficult to comprehend how a candidate who has a degree in social science, has never programmed before and is interested in making a career in the IT industry can understand the basic programming skills and answer the questions when attending these tests. Usually, no practice exercise is provided or sent to candidates. During these tests you are given a manual to read and understand how the instructions of the given assembly language operate and a booklet with questions to answer. Usually the answers require you to write a simple program of between 2 and 12 lines. The test is designed to test your logical ability to read and understand material on a new programming language quickly and to work under pressure, writing as many programs as possible correctly.

In this section you will learn a few basic rules regarding look-alike assembly language programming. The important and most common elements are presented, which will be useful for inexperienced candidates. To familiarize yourself and minimize mistakes during your actual tests, read the provided examples, tests and solutions at the end of this chapter. See how the programs are written using different instructions. But don't forget in your actual test to follow the given instruction set rules, which may differ from those in the examples given here.

Structure of assembly language

In the following test a number of fundamental characteristics, common to most assembly languages, will be introduced. We will use the following hypothetical microprocessor and associated assembly language which contains the following basic elements:

- Six storage registers A_0, A, B, C, D and E. A_0 is used only as a temporary storage register, either to store the integer from the keyboard using the instruction 'GetInt' or to display its content on the screen using the instruction 'ShoInt'. The A, B, C, D and E registers can be used to store variables, integers and constants. A full subset of the instruction set and its function operations used in this test are described in Table 3.1.

- Assembly language programs usually contain several passes of instructions; each one carries out a certain task. An example of an instruction and simple definitions using a single register A are shown below:

Endfile: MOV A, 3 ;Data transfer, which means A = 3

Endfile: is called a label. It is always separated by a colon (:) and is written to the far left of an instruction. You can choose any name for your label. Labels are usually used in conjunction with branch instructions such as JMP, JMPZ, JMPE, JNE, JLO and JGO. Their operation function is described in Table 3.1.

MOV is the instruction mnemonic. It means load or transfer the data from source (second operand), 3, to the destination (first operand), register A in the above example. Comments are always separated by a semicolon (;), and written to the far right of an instruction to explain the steps used to execute the program. Here they are used to help you annotate the program and understand the steps of execution. However, they are usually ignored during the actual tests, owing to the time limits.

Important note: The source (second operand) could be any variable, integer, constant or a register, but the destination (first operand) must always be a register. Also, only one variable, integer or constant may be operated on at a given time, using a single register. So 3M, for example, consists of two variables 3 and M, which should be operated on, or implemented, separately.

Table 3.1 A full subset of the instruction set and its function operations used in this test

Mnemonic	Function	Result
MOV	MOV A, 2	Load register A with 2, ie A = 2
	MOV I,10	Allocate I = 10
ADD	ADD A, 2	Add 2 to register A content , ie A = A + 2
	ADD A, B	Add A to B, ie A = A + B
SUB	SUB A, 2	Subtract 2 from register A content, ie A = A – 2
	SUB 2	Subtract the result in the last operation by 2
MUL	MUL A, 2	Multiply register A by 2, ie A = A × 2
DIV	DIV A, 2	Divide register A by 2, ie A = A/2
INC	INC A	Increment register A by one, ie A = A + 1
DEC	DEC A	Decrement register A by one, ie A = A – 1
CMP	CMP A, B	Compare the content of registers: A&B, ie A = B, A < B or A > B.
	CMP 2	Compare the result in the last operation with 2.
JMP	JMP	Causes an unconditional jump. It could be to a 'Label'
JMPZ	JMPZ	Jump if the result of an arithmetic operation in the last operation is zero
JMPE	JMPE	Jump if the result in the last operation produces an equal number
JNE	JNE	Jump if the result in the last operation produces a negative number
JLO	JLO	Jump if in the last operation the first operand was less than the second operand

Table 3.1 Continued

Mnemonic	Function	Result
JGO	JGO	Jump if in the last operation the first operand was greater than the second operand
GetInt	GetInt	Get an integer from the keyboard and store it in register A_0
ShoInt	ShoInt	Display the contents of register A_0 on the screen

Tips

As mentioned before, these tests tend to be easy if you have some programming skills. However, the examples below and the test solutions provided are a very good way to start familiarizing yourself. I cannot recommend any particular book because most are written for a specific CPU architecture; nevertheless, it may help you to look at one (it doesn't matter which) to see the extensive list of instructions.

In most of these tests you are required to perform simple mathematical operations, including counting and looping, and to follow simple rules:

- Simplify algebraic expressions by performing the operations inside parentheses first and reduce a fraction to the lowest possible terms, ie the numerator and denominator have no common factors, before writing your program; eg 8/12 + 8/6 = 24/12 = 2. This final result should be used in your program.
- Multiplication/division must be programmed first, then addition or subtraction.

- Usually, a single storage register is allowed to store only one operand at a time. Therefore, before performing any mathematical operation using the second operand, make sure which operand you should express first, as shown in the example below:

  eg ADD A, B ;A = A + B

  ADD B, A ;B = B + A

- Usually the instruction 'CMP' is followed by a jump instruction. Use different jump instructions depending on the question requirements. Also, use register A_0 only to get an integer from the keyboard or to display its content on the screen. You might also find other restrictions in your actual test.

A brief illustration of these basic instruction rules is provided in the examples below.

Example 1

```
        MOV   A, 6           ;A = 6
        ADD   A, 4           ;A = 6 + 4 = 10
        INC   A              ;A = A + 1 = 10 + 1 = 11
        DEC   A              ;A = A – 1 = 11 – 1 = 10
        SUB   A, 6           ;A = A – 6 = 10 – 6 = 4
        MOV   B, 8           ;B = 8
        ADD   A, B           ;A = A + B = 4 + 8 = 12
        SUB   A, B           ;A = A – B = 12 – 8 = 4
JMP     Finish               ;The program will jump to the
                             ;label called Finish and leave the
                             ;rest of the program
End:    MOV   Result, 0      ;Result = 0
        ADD   Result, A      ;Result = Result + A = 0 + 12 = 12
        SUB   B, Result      ;B = B – Result = 8 – 12 = –4
```

```
Finish:  ADD   A, B        ;A = A + B = 4 + 8 = 12
         JMP   End         ;The program will jump back to
the
                           ;label called End.
```

Example 2

Write a program using the basic commands described in Table 3.1 to evaluate the arithmetical expression 10 + (12 – 4), first by using a single register (ie A); second by using two registers (ie A and B), leaving the results in register A.

First, using a single register:

```
         MOV   A, 12       ;A = 12
         SUB   A, 4        ;A = A – 4 = 12 – 4 = 8
         ADD   A, 10       ;A = A + 10 = 8 + 10 = 18
```

Second, using two registers

```
         MOV   A, 12       ;A = 12
         MOV   B, 4        ;B = 4
         SUB   A, B        ;A = A – B = 12 – 4 = 8
         ADD   A, 10       ;A = A + 10 = 8 + 10 = 18
```

You might sometimes be asked to start your program with 'BEGIN' and finish with 'END' or 'HLT' to terminate the program execution. Since we are using a hypothetical assembly language, this is considered to be a decorative rather than a necessary operation, and in the following tests is not required. But you may have to use it in your actual test.

Now imagine that you have been invited to sit an IT computer aptitude test. Carefully read again the structure of the assembly language test, understand the basic functions of the operation instructions in Table 3.1 meticulously and study the fundamental rules stated in 'Tips' thoroughly for 30 minutes. Then try the following 14 questions and see how many programs you can write in 30 minutes:

1. Implement the following mathematical equations in assembly language using registers A and B.

   I = 1
   I = I + 12
   J = 6

   Then store the result (I + J) in register A.
2. Implement the following expressions in assembly language using registers A, B and C.

   I = 10
   I = I + 4
   X = 9
   Y = X – I

3. Implement the following instructions in assembly language using registers A and B.

   X = 2
   If X – Y = 0 Then X = X + 1
   Otherwise Y = Y + 1

4. Write a program which causes a jump to an instruction labelled ZERO if the value of the variable COUNT is zero or to an instruction labelled EQUAL if the value of the variable COUNT is equal to100. Otherwise to an instruction labelled OTHER using single register A.
5. Evaluate the following equation using two registers, A and B

   $(3 + 5)/(15 - 3)/(4/3) + (9/4) - (11/8) \times X = 0$

6. Write a program to evaluate the following expression using two registers, A and B.
   {((11 – 2)/3) X + (6 * 3/9) – I)} Y
7. Compare two variables stored in registers A and B. If they are equal then add 20 to A and subtract 5 from B. If they are not equal then add 2 to A and subtract 2 from B.
8. Multiply two numbers, ie NUM1 and NUM2, by 4 and put the results in register A and B respectively.
9. Write a program to sum sequences 2, 4, 6, 8, 10 up to 30. Store the results in a variable called TOTAL-SUM, using registers A and B.
10. Write a program to sum the integers 1 to 30 by an increment of 1 every time and store the result in a variable called SUM, using registers A and B.
11. Write a program to add 15 consecutive numbers from 20 to 34 inclusive. Use registers A and B and accumulate the results in register C.
12. Write a program using the instruction 'GetInt' to input two integers X and Y from the keyboard to calculate (X – Y)(X + Y). Then use the instruction 'ShoInt' to display the result on the screen using registers A, B, C and D.
13. Write a program to input two integers from the keyboard and display the smaller one. Use registers A and B.
14. Write a program where the positive integers are added to register A until a negative integer is input. Then display the sum of the numbers. Use registers A and B.

Spatial concepts

In this test you are often provided with the net of a benchmark unfolded box with a different pattern on each side. Your task is to build a three-dimensional image of the box. Then you have to compare the box from different angles and views with a set of boxes, decide which of these boxes matches the benchmark box, and mark your answer. Of course, you have to twist and turn the box in different directions in order to be able to visualize the whole pattern. In this book I have presented you with four methods of visualizing the three-dimensional box by twisting and rotating the sides around the two identified bases as shown in Figures 3.1, 3.2, 3.3 and 3.4 and their solutions. The dotted line indicates the formation of the box around the two bases from two different angles sufficient to visualize the shape of the box. Study all the diagrams carefully. Copy one or all of the given diagrams and try to build a box, and see how the patterns are arranged from different angles. Remember, a box always has six sides.

Tips

- First, identify the two bases (B) of the unfolded box and always use them as a benchmark to compare and view the other given boxes. Then follow one of the four methods presented in this book to build up the three-dimensional box. Twisting and rotating the sides by 90, 180 and 360 degrees towards the two identified bases will show you how the box will look if it is folded from different angles. In this way you will able to visualize how the pattern on each side is adjusted in relation to a different base from different angles.
- I recommend that in your test you spend a couple of seconds drawing a very quick and simple draft of what the

shape of the folded box would look like from the view angle of the two bases before you start answering the questions. In this way you will be assured that your answers will be correct, and it will save time and avoid unnecessary confusion.

- Different sizes and shapes of boxes may be used, eg rectangular for all sides, two sides wider than the other four sides, etc. The methods used in this book always hold; try to see this for yourself. Again, identify the bases and then rotate the sides towards each base to form a three-dimensional shape from different angles.

Figure 3.1 Net

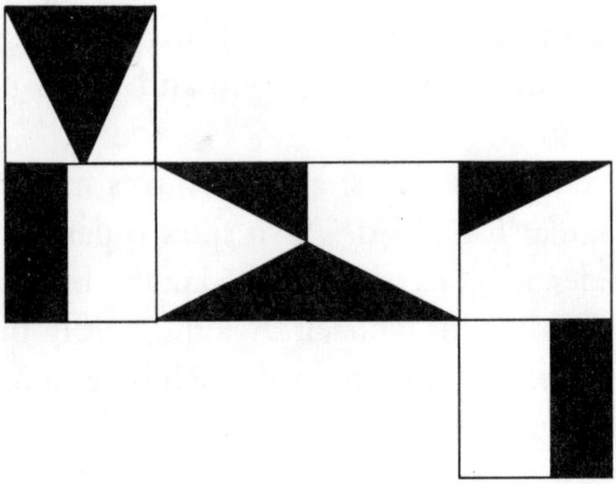

Figure 3.1 Three-dimensional solution

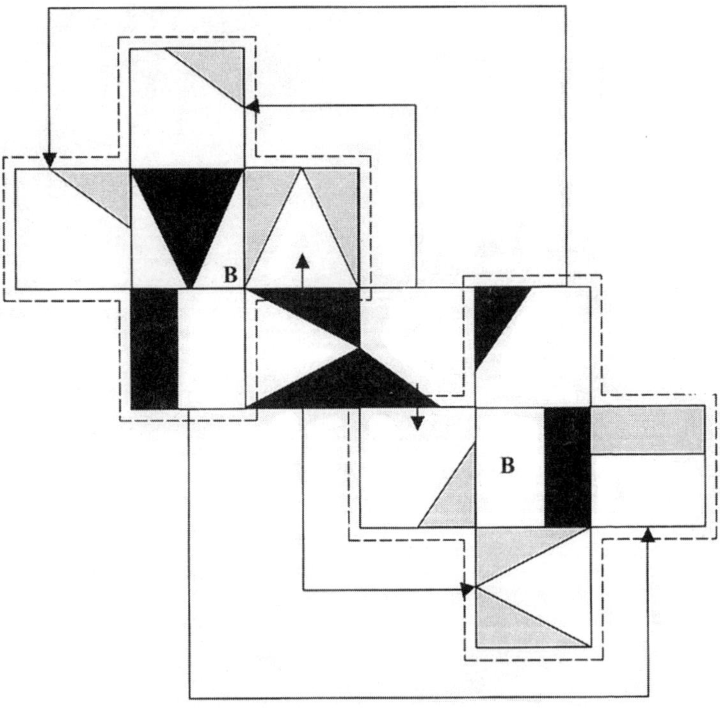

Figure 3.2 Net

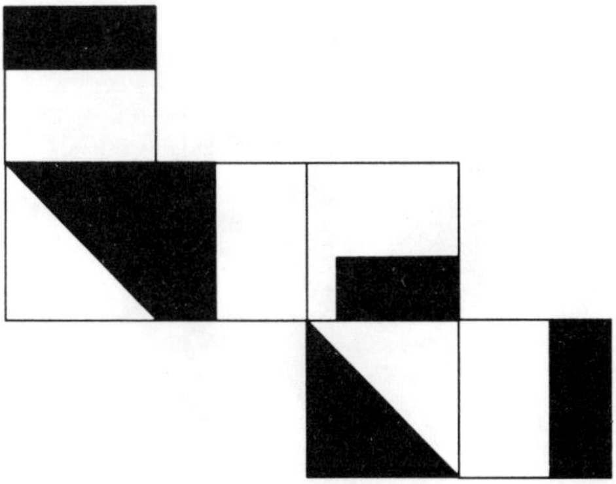

Figure 3.2 Three-dimensional solution

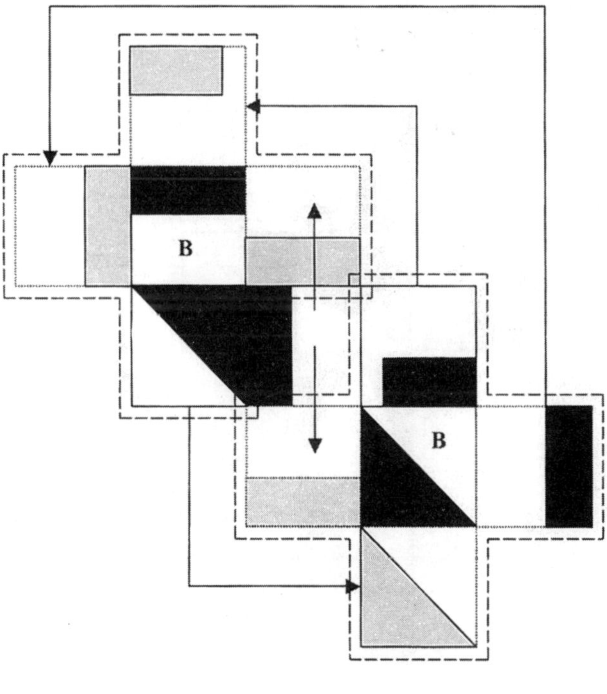

Figure 3.3 Net

Figure 3.3 Three-dimensional solution

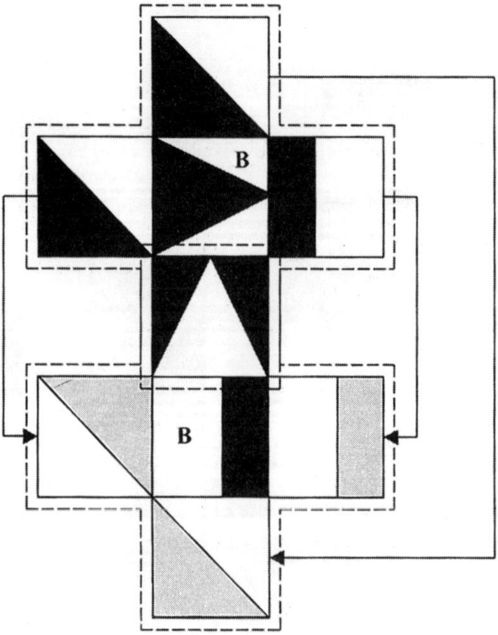

Figure 3.4 Net

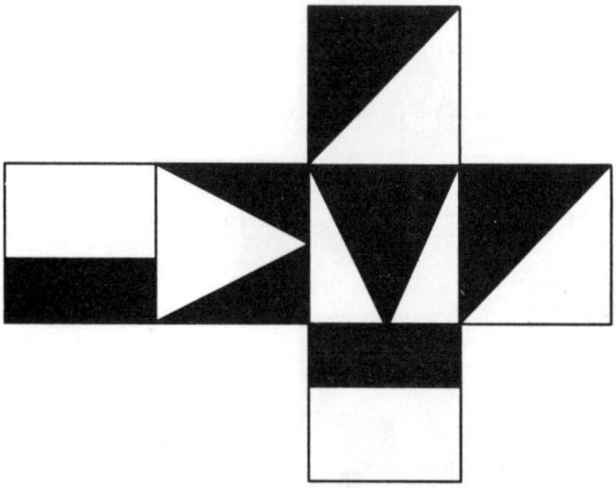

Figure 3.4 Three-dimensional solution

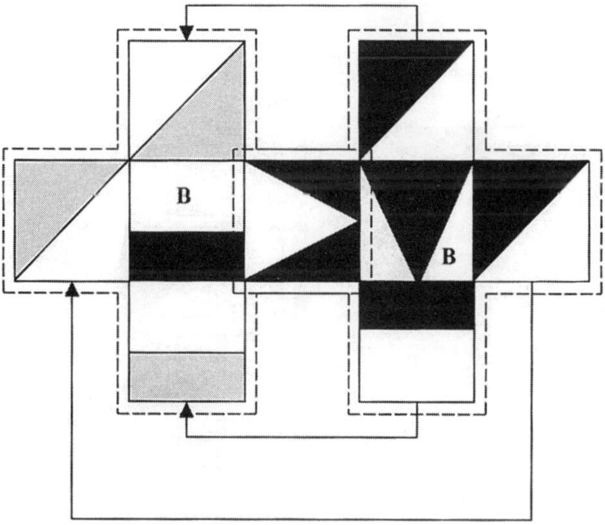

Now, look at Figure 3.5 and see how many of the associated questions in Figure 3.6 you can complete in 3 minutes. Compare your results with the answers given at the end of this chapter. To help you with this exercise I have provided the three-dimensional solution.

Figure 3.5 Net exercise

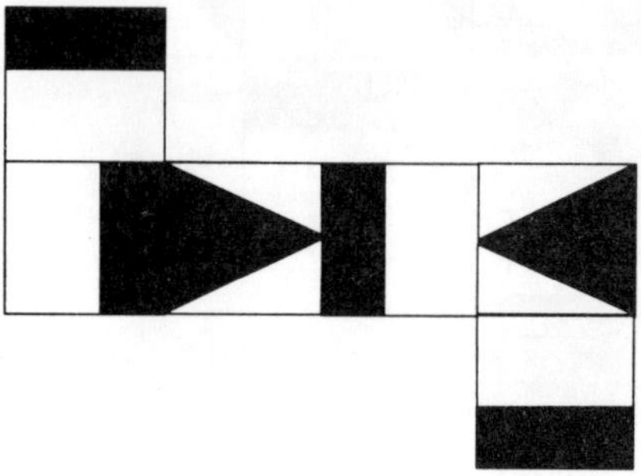

Figure 3.5 Three-dimensional solution

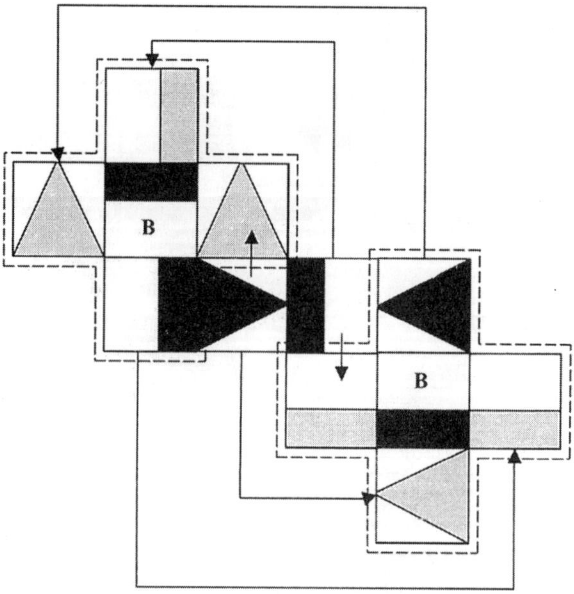

Figure 3.6

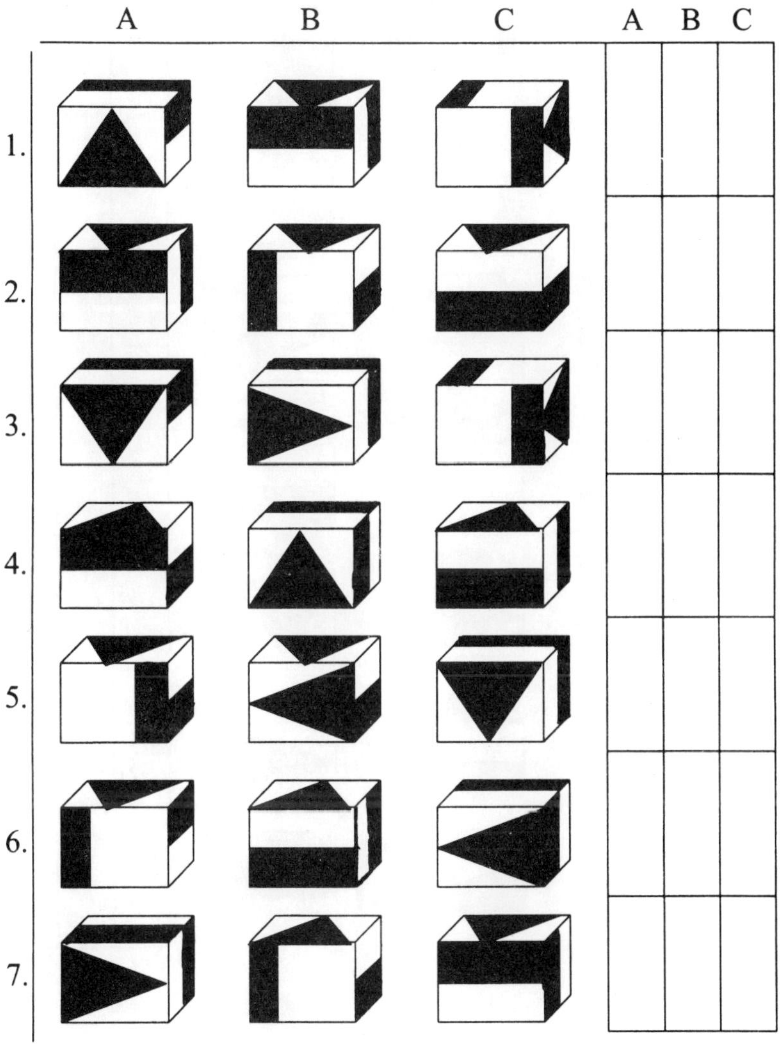

	A	B	C	A	B	C
8.						
9.	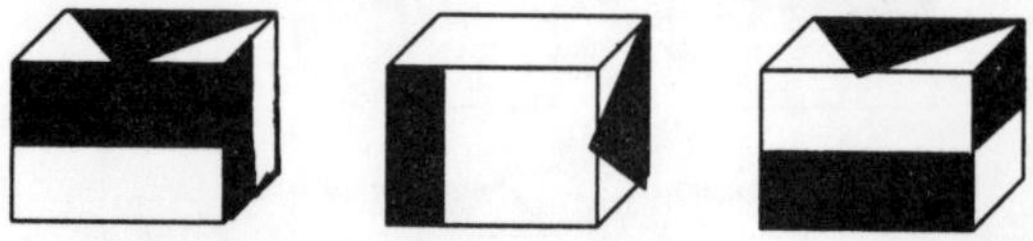					
10.						
11.						
12.						
13.						
14.	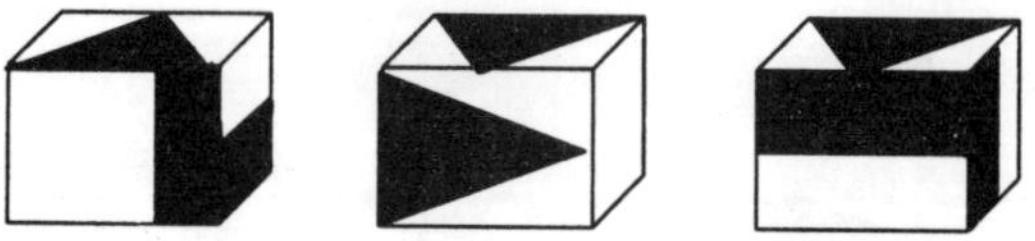					

Answers to practice exercises

Solutions to high-level programming language test

Compiler checking by tracking error

1. SE
2. NE
3. OE
4. SE, LE
5. SE
6. OE
7. LE
8. SE
9. SE, OE
10. SE, OE
11. SE, OE
12. NE
13. SE
14. NE
15. SE
16. NE
17. SE
18. LE
19. SE, LE, OE
20. SE, OE
21. SE, LE, OE
22. SE, LE
23. OE
24. SE, OE
25. NE
26. LE
27. SE, LE, OE

28. OE
29. LE
30. SE, LE
31. NE
32. NE
33. OE
34. SE
35. SE, OE
36. SE, OE
37. NE
38. LE
39. NE
40. NE
41. LE, OE

Compiler checking by line rules

1. Z
2. Y
3. X, Y
4. X
5. Y
6. X, Y
7. Z
8. W
9. W
10. W, Y
11. X, Y
12. Y
13. Z
14. X, Y
15. Z
16. W
17. Z

18. Z
19. X, Y
20. W, Y
21. W, X
22. W
23. Y
24. Z
25. W
26. Z
27. W, X
28. W, X, Y
29. W
30. Z
31. Z
32. W
33. W
34. W
35. Z
36. W
37. X, Y
38. X
39. W
40. W, Y

Spatial concepts

1. A
2. C
3. B
4. C
5. C
6. B
7. C
8. A

9. A
10. C
11. C
12. A
13. C
14. C

Solutions for assembly language test

1.		MOV	A, I	;A = 1
		ADD	A, 12	;A = A + 12 = I + 12 = 1 + 12 = 13
		MOV	B, J	;B = J = 6
		ADD	A, B	;A = A + B = 13 + 6 = 19
2.		MOV	A, I	;A = I = 10
		ADD	A, 4	;A = A + 4 = 10 + 4 = 14
		MOV	B, X	;B = X = 9
		SUB	B, A	;B = B – A = X – A = 9 – 14 = –5
		MOV	C, Y	;C = Y
		MOV	C, B	;C = Y = B = X – A = –5
3.		MOV	A, X	;A = X = 2
		MOV	B, Y	;B = Y
		SUB	A, B	;A = A – B = X – Y = 2 – Y
		JMPZ	Next	; If X – Y = 0 then jump to label Next
		INC	B	; Otherwise, if X – Y = 0 then Y = Y + 1
	Next:	INC	A	; X = X + 1
4.		MOV	A, COUNT	;A = COUNT
		JMPZ	ZERO	;If COUNT = 0, go to ZERO
		CMP	100	;Compare COUNT with 100

```
        JMPE   EQUAL       ;If COUNT = 100 then go to
                           EQUAL

        JMP    OTHER       ;Otherwise go to OTHER
ZERO:
EQUAL:
OTHER:
```

5. After simplifying algebraic expressions you get:

22 – 11 X = 0

```
        MOV    A, 11       ;A = 11
        MUL    A, X        ;A = 11 X
        MOV    B, 22       ;B = 22
        SUB    B, A        ;B = B – A = 22 – 11 X
        MOV    B, 0        ;B = 0 = 22 – 11X
```

6. After simplifying algebraic expressions you get:

{3X + (2 – I)} Y

```
        MOV    A, 2        ;A = 2
        SUB    A, I        ;A = 2 – I
        MOV    B, 3        ;B = 3
        MUL    B, X        ;B = 3X
        ADD    B, A        ;B = B + A = 3X + (2 – I)
        MUL    B, Y        ;B = {3X + (2 – I)}Y
```

7.

```
        CMP    A, B        ;Compare the content of
                           registers A&B
               Both-Equal  ;If A = B then go to Both-
        JMPE               Equal
                                  ;Otherwise
        ADD    A, 2        ;A = A + 2;
        SUB    B, 2        ;B = B – 2,
```

```
Both-Equal: ADD  A, 20        ;A = A + 20
            SUB  B, 5         ;B = B – 5
8.          MOV  A, NUM1      ;A = NUM1
            ADD  A, A         ;A = A + A = 2A
            ADD  A, A         ;A = 2A + 2A = 4A

            MOV  B, NUM2      ;B = NUM2
            ADD  B, B         ;B = 2B
            ADD  B, B         ;B = 4B
9.          MOV  A, TOTAL     ;A = TOTAL-SUM
                 -SUM
            MUL  A, 0         ;A = TOTAL-SUM = 0
            MOV  B, 2         ;Set the counter using
                              register B = 2
Repeat:     CMP  B, 30        ;If B = 30, then
            JMPE Finish       ;Go to label Finish
                              ;Otherwise
            ADD  A, B         ;TOTAL-SUM = A = A
                              + B = 0 + 2 = 2
            ADD  B, 2         ;B = B + 2 = 2 + 2 = 4
            JMP  Repeat       ;Continue adding until
                              you reach 30
Finish:

10.         MOV  A, SUM       ;A = SUM
            MOV  A, 0         ;A = 0
            MOV  B, 1         ;Set the counter B = 1

Repeat:     CMP  B, 30
            JMPE Finish       ;If B = 30 go to Label
                              Finish
                              ;Otherwise
            ADD  A, B         ;A = SUM = SUM + B
                              = 0 + 1
```

```
            INC   B            ;B = B + 1 = 1 + 1 = 2
            JMP   Repeat       ;Continue adding 1 to
                               30
    Finish:
11. Begin:  MOV   A, 15        ;Initiate a counter
            MOV   B, 20        ;Start value, B = 20
            MOV   C, 0         ;C = 0

    Repeat: ADD   C, B         ;C = C + B = 0 + 20
            INC   B            ;B = B + 1 = 20 + 1 = 21
            SUB   A, 1         ;A = A – 1 = 15 – 1 = 14
            JGO   Repeat       ;Go to Repeat if A>1
12.         GetInt             ;Get an Integer from the
                               keyboard and store A0
            MOV   A, A0        ;Store the first value = X
                               in register A
            GetInt             ;Get the second Integer
                               from the keyboard
            MOV   B, A0        ;Store the second value
                               = Y in register B
            MOV   C, A         ;C = X
            ADD   C, B         ;C = C + B = X + Y
            MOV   D, A         ;D = A = X
            SUB   D, B         ;D = D – B = X – Y
            MUL   C, D         ;C = C × D = (X + Y)(X
                               – Y)
            MOV   A0, C        ;Transfer the content of
                               register C to A0
            ShoInt             ;This command will
                               display the content of A0
13.         GetInt             ;Get first integer and
                               store it in register A0
            MOV   A, A0        ;Store the first integer in
                               register A
```

```
           GetInt            ;Get the second integer
                             and store it in A0
           MOV  B, A0        ;Store the second integer
                             in register B
           CMP  B, A         ;Compare the first and
                             second integer
           JLO  Loop1        ;Jump if the integer in
                             register A < B
           ShoInt            ;Display the second
                             integer
           JMP  Loop2        ;Unconditional jump to
                             Loop2 if needed
Loop1:     MOV  A0, A        ;Otherwise transfer the
                             first integer into A0
           ShoInt            ;Display the first integer
Loop2:
```

14.

```
           MOV  A, 0         ;Clear register A = 0
Loop1:     GetInt            ;Get an integer from
                             keyboard and store in A0
           MOV  B, A0        ;Transfer the input
                             integer to register B
           JNE  Loop2        ;Jump to Loop2 if the
                             input integer is negative
           ADD  A, B         ;A = A + B
           JMP  Loop1        ;Unconditional jump to
                             Loop1
Loop2:     MOV  A0, B        ;Transfer the content of
                             B ready for display
           ShoInt            ;Display the content of
                             A0
```

4

Common verbal reasoning tests

Verbal reasoning tests

There are a variety of verbal reasoning tests, such as missing words tests, word swapping tests, hidden sentences tests, spelling tests, sentence completion tests, sentence correction tests, grammatical tests, sentence sequence tests, analytical writing tests, data sufficient tests, identifying words having the same or opposite meaning tests, verbal critical reasoning tests (VCR) and others. All these tests specialize in testing certain uses of the English language. However, after contacting various organizations big and small, and contacting many graduates and professionals who applied for jobs in management, finance and IT, I found that critical verbal reasoning is the most popular and widely used, especially for management and finance recruitment, where reading documents or producing concise and meaningful materials or writing reports and letters plays a major part in the job requirement. However, for IT recruitment it depends on the positions the company are recruiting for. Take, for example, programming positions; the tests provided in Chapter 3 in this book are mainly used. However, assessment for other IT positions may include VCR tests as well as other tests from this book. Therefore I will here concentrate only on VCR tests.

The principal objective of the verbal reasoning tests is to test skills in understanding, evaluating and analysing argument in written verbally complex passages and drawing logical conclusions between what the writer is implying in the claim and what is actually stated. The passages are followed by a number of statements and your task is to decide whether each statement is True or False (from the information given in the passage) or Can't Tell (because further information is needed to support the claim). Ambiguity occurs when the meanings of words, phrases or statements are easily confused with actual assumptions in the passage. To make the test more difficult the subject of the passage and statements is usually a hot topic in the public domain, on which you may have prior knowledge and have formed a particular opinion. VCR tests a comprehensive understanding of the English language (which is beyond the scope of this book) and most of the skills mentioned above are needed indirectly in order to be able to analyse the information logically and answer the questions correctly.

Tips

- Reading of various papers, books, technical manuals and magazines would be a good start. However, you also need to develop your vocabulary, including synonyms and antonyms, using a thesaurus or any other resources. You should also be able to question the facts: What is the writer's purpose or intent in making this claim? Is there a hidden message between the lines? Does the relationship between words or sentences make sense?
- Familiarizing yourself with jargon words in your subject speciality is needed, because often the assumptions on which the argument is built are concealed in the meaning of words.

- Always look at cue words in the passages such as 'if', 'since', 'because' and so on, which usually identify the reason or premise in support of the writer's claim.
- Never, ever, in your tests draw any conclusion based on your prior knowledge of the subject in the passage. Always confine yourself to the information given in the passage. Don't forget that all the information you need to make a decision is in the passage alone and that there is only one solution.
- Be careful when you see absolute words such as 'ever', 'all', 'always', 'definitely' and so on in the statement. Most of the time the answer is False or Can't Tell.
- Look out for words that are similar in meaning such as 'propound' and 'propose'; 'revamp' and 'renovate'; 'undignified' and 'unceremonious'; 'least profitable' and 'modest profit'; 'paradoxically' and 'in contrast'; and so on. They might appear sequentially in the passage and statement to confuse you.
- Be aware of words that sound alike such as 'sight' and 'site'; 'horde' and 'hoard'; 'in' and 'inn'; 'precede' and 'proceed'; and so on. Make sure you understand their different meanings.

Critical verbal reasoning tests

In this test, you are given eight passages. For each passage you are provided with a number of statements. Your task is to read each passage carefully and analyse and evaluate the given information logically, then choose one answer according to the rules given below:

- If the statement is True, write Capital **T**.
- If the statement is False, write Capital **F**.
- If you Can't tell whether the statement is true or false because there isn't sufficient information to support the claim, write capital **C**.

You have 15 minutes to complete the test; start when you are ready.

British scientists using wireless communication are working on the next generation of all-terrain robotic explorers for Mars that will be able to go to regions where satellite images suggest that water once flowed or might still remain underground. Water is considered essential for the evolution of life and some scientists believe they have evidence, from a Martian rock, that the planet once had life. The big difference between the new all-terrain robot and Pathfinder which was sent earlier is that it can move on sandy slopes with 50-degree slants, and even reconfigure parts of its body to maintain its balance as it rolls over rough terrain, using cameras, sensors and new control software.

1. The main difference between the new and old robot to explore Mars is its agility.
2. The new all-terrain robots are able of controlling themselves in such a way that they will be able to access and fully traverse the water region.
3. The concept of life throughout the universe will be accepted, if water is found on Mars.

The two-year study by the respected Swedish Radiation and Nuclear Safety Authority suggests a potential new risk to health from mobile phones, with the discovery that their radiation emission can damage human cells. It found that the critical factor determining the radiation emissions was the length between the earpiece and the mobile phone antenna. However, researchers said that the findings were not strong enough to cast serious doubt on the safety of mobile phones. Cells in culture often behave differently from those in living tissue, and the study offers no evidence of adverse effect.

4. If someone is worried about radiation levels they should adopt a precautionary approach and limit the length of time they use a mobile phone.
5. The Swedish Radiation and Nuclear Safety Authority has proposed that mobile phones can be a risk to your health.
6. Blood vessel cells cultured in the laboratory usually behave abnormally when bombarded with emissions even when they are within safety guidelines for mobile phones.
7. Hands-free wiring reduces radiation.
8. Mobile users have an increased health risk.

A confessed student cheater says that academic pressure has made cheating a way to survive in universities. The better grades you have, the better job you get, the better you're going to do in life. And if you learn to cut corners to do that, you're going to be saving yourself time and energy. The Education Authority lamented the changes in universities' culture where grades and test scores are more important than integrity. It seems that honour is a concept of the past.

9. The Education Authority welcomed the changes in universities' culture.
10. Students sometimes cheat due to academic pressure.
11. In the real world cheating is going to be acceptable, because it's how well you do that shows, not how morally you do it.

12. Honour is a concept of the past and students should do anything in order to succeed.
13. Only grades and scores decide one's future job prospects.

Most modern computers are designed using the 'Von Neumann' architecture and built using silicon transistor technology. The size of the transistors on silicon chips has continued to decrease dramatically. But we're approaching the limits, because this will make the design expensive and also affect the packing density, speed of performance and hence the functionality, since increasing miniaturization reduces capacitance and interconnection length. As a result, it may be that progress with silicon technology ceases on economic grounds before the absolute physical limit is reached. In any case, the challenge is to find alternative technologies, and it is highly possible that these will be based on quantum mechanics to replace the new generation of microprocessor chips.

14. Only reduction in capacitance can be expected in the miniaturization of silicon chips.
15. Computer chips designed using 'Von Neumann' architecture are more likely to be replaced by quantum mechanics.
16. Silicon chips are a widely used technology in all old-generation microprocessors.
17. In the future quantum mechanics will definitely replace the current silicon technology.

The National Hurricane Centre monitors the ocean and determines that a weather disturbance is a tropical storm when it has winds above 50-mph. A tropical storm is upgraded to a hurricane when its winds climb higher than 75-mph. A normal season averages 10 named storms in the Atlantic, but last year, 15 named storms occurred. The strength of a tropical storm can depend on how tightly the storm clouds are formed in the centre.

18. The strength of a hurricane can depend on how tightly the rotation storm clouds are formed around the eye of the storm.
19. If the wind has a speed of above 80-km a disturbance is upgraded to a tropical storm.
20. No more than 10 named storms hit the Atlantic every year.
21. The general public are always warned when a hurricane is in the area.

One-fifth of EU countries' population is aged 65 or older. In roughly the last 30 years, the growth in dual-earner families has grown by 30 per cent. Single-parent families have increased, too, in the same period of around 1968 to 2002. Most of these single-parent families are headed by women, but there's a high growth rate among men leading single-parent families as well.

22. Most of the single-parent families in the UK are headed by women.
23. About 80 per cent of the EU population is under 65 years old.
24. Single-parent families in the EU usually get government support.
25. In the last 30 years the number of married couples where both spouses work has dropped in the EU.
26. Married couples with families are more stressed because of their career.

The US surgeon-general last December warned that more than 61 per cent of Americans are considered obese, and obesity accounts for 300,000 deaths a year – putting it in the same league as tobacco. Obesity-related costs have reached an estimated $113bn annually. Treating related conditions such as diabetes and heart failure absorbs nearly 8 per cent of health spending. Suing food-makers would be tricky. Food, unlike cigarettes, is not inherently harmful or addictive. Proving in court the link between a plaintiff's heart disease and a particular food is a big challenge. The solution to the problem, says Betsy Jones, chief-executive *of a big food company, is education, balance, variety and moderation (in eating) and people undertaking physical activity.*

27. The public must be educated to control obesity.
28. No one can really be sure if someone is ill because of obesity.
29. Cigarettes and food are major health hazards that cannot be traced to the act of any human or organization.
30. The US government earns millions of dollars from food tax and tens of thousands of civilians are employed in the food industry.
31. Winning litigation against the food industry wouldn't be as difficult as in the tobacco industry.
32. Food will always be the main contributor to obesity.

Owing to the downturn in the IT market the FTSE suffered a sharp downturn of 11 per cent on Tuesday after falling to 3860.3, its lowest point since September 1996. A drop in the stock market below 3500 is highly possible, but not likely. On Monday, Europe's most valuable stock market index dropped 5.4 per cent, its biggest one-day percentage fall since a 5.7 per cent loss on 11 September 2001. The Bank of England expected the nation's economy to grow 2.5 per cent and unemployment to fall to 1.5 per cent this year and between 1.5 and 1.3 per cent respectively in 2003.

33. With slow growth in economy and high uncertainties, the Bank of England is likely to keep its target for a key short-term interest rate low until economic recovery seems more likely.
34. The UK economy will definitely grow by 2.5% this year.
35. The downturn in the UK stock market is due to 11 September.
36. The Bank of England expects that unemployment will drop by 0.2% in 2003 as compared with 2002.

Answers to practice exercises

1.	T	19.	T
2.	T	20.	F
3.	C	21.	C
4.	C	22.	C
5.	F	23.	T
6.	C	24.	C
7.	C	25.	F
8.	F	26.	C
9.	F	27.	T
10.	T	28.	T
11.	C	29.	F
12.	F	30.	C
13.	F	31.	F
14.	F	32.	C
15.	F	33.	C
16.	C	34.	F
17.	C	35.	C
18.	T	36.	T

5

Common numerical psychometric tests

Introduction

All candidates applying for IT, finance and management jobs have to take a numerical test, to test their abilities to work with numbers. In this book I present three kinds of test which are widely used and which deal with basic principles of arithmetic (addition, subtraction, multiplication and division). Knowledge of mathematical terminology, symbols and processes such as percentage, ratio, roots, decimals, fractions, powers and exponents is usually required. Therefore, brush up your maths skills and consult your old maths books because the basics are not covered here. The first and second sections of this chapter deal with estimation calculation and problem solving worked out without the use of a calculator. However, in section 3, which deals with the data interpretation of tables and graphs, you are free to use one. I urge you throughout this chapter to look at the given answer before working on the problem, to give you an idea of what you should expect and help you to exclude unreasonable alternatives.

Numerical estimation

In this test you are presented with a variety of questions to which you must estimate the answer. Quick mental arithmetic can be done using scrap paper. However, in a real test you would have no time. Therefore try to practise and familiarize yourself with these types of problem. Always keep in mind that you are never asked to supply an exact answer for the question; you are only asked to estimate which of the given choices is closest.

Tips

To give you practice in avoiding common mistakes:

- If you have to multiply/divide and add/subtract do the multiplication/division first as in this example:

  $20 - 5 + 9 \times 5 \div 5 = 20 - 5 + 45 \div 5 = 20 - 5 + 9 = 24$

- If you have to divide and multiply by the same number, then don't bother; the result is always one, as shown below:

  $(10 \div 5)\ 5 = 10$ or $20 + 5 \times 15 \div 15 = 25$

- Use quick mental arithmetic, for example:

292 + 398 + 102 + 801	A	B	C	D
	1598	1593	1590	1597

  The quick mental arithmetic 300 + 400 +100 + 800 gives a result of 1600; therefore all the suggested answers A, B, C, D appear possible at first. However, if you add the remaining unit numbers you get –8 – 2 + 2 + 1= –7. So only B can be the right answer, since 1600 – 7 = 1593.

- Allocate your time effectively and leave the difficult questions for later to sort out if you still have time left.

Another way to provide an erudite numeracy recreation and develop your quick mental arithmetic skills is the MasterMaths game as shown below. By continuously playing the game, the basic mathematical principles will be embedded in your brain to be used in your daily life or in your numeracy psychometric tests.

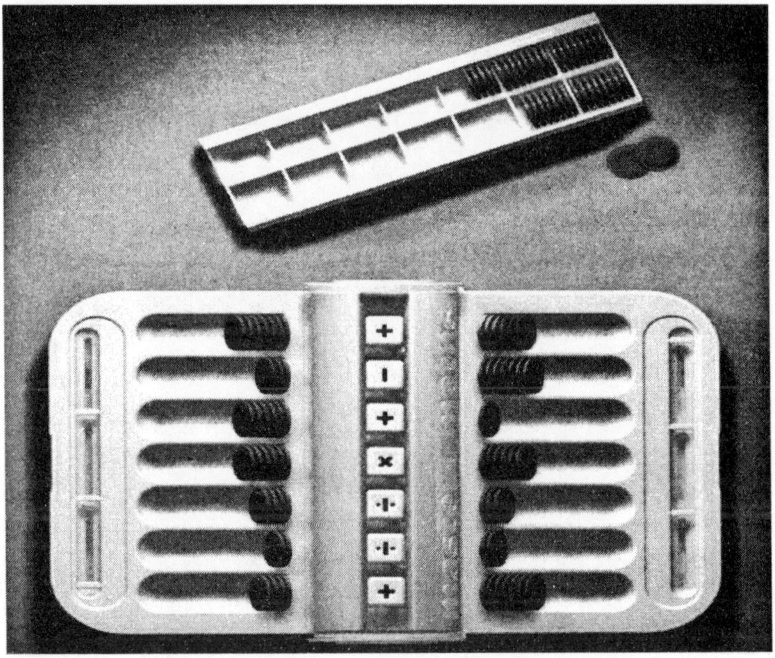

Now try the test in Table 5.1, which consists of 30 questions that must be answered within a time limit of 7 minutes. The questions range from very easy to quite challenging.

Table 5.1 Numerical estimation test

	A	B	C	D
1. 304 ÷ 2 + 15 – 25 = ?	138	142	135	145
2. 4 + 6 × 2 ÷ 2 × 1 + 3 – 5 = ?	8	6	5	10
3. 9 ¼ + 10 ¾ – 2 3/2 + 2.5 = ?	18	17	19	21
4. 6 2/4 ÷ ½ × 4/2 = ?	7.5	7	6	6.5
5. 9/3 × 75/5 ÷ 4/12 × 48/2 + 5/10 × 20/4 – 5 = ?	4	3	5	6
6. ½ + 2/6 + 7/4 + 9/2 – 8/2 = ?	6	4	3	5
7. 7 + 6.241 + 18.021 + 2.2 = ?	29	30	35	33
8. 8.1 + 2.33 + 9.001 + 16.02 = ?	35	37	33	31
9. 5.020 – 1.112 – 1.021 – 0.38 = ?	2.8	2.5	2.9	2.7
10. (7.5 + 55)/(0.05) + 10 = ?	1270	1255	1260	1250
11. (82 – 0.44)/(2.002) + 15 = ?	54	56	58	59
12. 20% + 15% + 65% + 1 = ?	2	1	3	1.5
13. 13% × 2/65 + 10 = ?	9.5	10.5	11	10
14. 50% × 120/50 + 300/100 + 100% – 2 = ?	3.8	3	4	4.5
15. 7 + 58 + (–4) + 8 – (–5) = ?	74	73	75	72
16. –2 + (–6.2) – (–0.2) – (–5) = ?	+3	–4	+4	–3
17. –5.8 + 3 + (–2.18) – (–10.06) + (–1.08) = ?	–4	4	3.5	–3.5
18. –10 + 19 – (–2) + (–3) + (+2) = ?	10.5	9	10	11
19. (–3) (+2) + (–10) (–2) – (+2) (+4) = ?	6	–2	5	–3
20. (–9) (–2) + (–8) (–6) – (–5) (–4) = ?	–46	46	–12	40
21. 5426 – 3202 + 236 – 980 = ?	–1480	1485	1475	1480
22. 9302 + 2105 – 9003 + 12 = ?	2419	–2420	2416	2418
23. 120½ + 180¾ – 50 1/5 – 2 4/5 = ?	248	245	249	250
24. 12 2/5 – 19¾ + 6 6/5 + 3 3/2 = ?	4 7/25	4 9/20	4 5/18	4 7/20
25. –23 + 73 9/6 + 19 – 22 5/4 = ?	49	47 9/6	46 5/4	52
26. √25 + √36 – √144 = ?	13	+1	–1	0
27. 3 v25 + 3 v9 – 5 v49 = ?	–11	10	–35	15
28. 2 √36 – 10 √9 + 3 √25 – 2 √49 = ?	17	–17	15	–15
29. $8^{1/3} + 25^{½} + 9^{½} – 2$ = ?	10	9	7	8
30. $2^{1/3} + 125^{1/3} – 512^{1/3}$ = ?	3	0	–1	1

Problem solving

This test requires, as well as the knowledge of mathematical principles, an understanding of the fundamentals of algebra and arithmetic.

Tip

As they say, understanding the question is half the answer. Therefore read carefully and make sure you know what is required of you. Avoid making assumptions about costs rising, etc. Use only the information given in the question. Try quick mental arithmetic if possible. Also practise the mathematical operations presented in the previous section as well as others such as averages, fractions etc, which are useful for this section before you start the test. Nearly all of the questions are easily answered once you have figured out how the question works. Don't perform unnecessary calculations if you can use quick mental calculations. The time you save can be used to check other questions.

The following test will give you the necessary confidence for the real test in order to avoid unnecessary mistakes.

Now try the test below, which consists of 21 questions that must be answered within a time limit of 9 minutes.

1. How much will it cost to build a wall round a house that is 25 metres long and 75 metres wide, if the cost of 50 cm is £10?

A	B	C
£4,000	£40,000	400

2. It costs a publisher *n* pounds for each book to publish the first 1,000 books; extra books cost *n*/6 pound each. How many pounds will it cost to publish 7,000 books?

A	B	C
$7000n$	$2000n$	$5000n$

3. The distance between London and Hull is 300 miles. An Intercity train travels at 120 miles per hour from London to Hull. The train then goes back to London. If the total journey time was 4 hours and 30 minutes, what was the average speed of the Intercity train on the way back to London?

A	B	C
160 mph	140 mph	150 mph

4. At weekends the local Bowling club charges each person a flat rate of n pounds for up to 3 hours and $1/9n$ for each hour or fraction of an hour after the first 3 hours. How much does it cost for 2 people to go for 6 hours and 25 minutes at the weekend?

A	B	C
$6/9n$	$26/9n$	$13/9n$

5. John bought £3,000 worth of stocks in company X. He sold 2/3 of his stock after the value doubled, then sold the remaining stock at 4 times its purchase price. What was the total profit on the stock of company X?

A	B	C
£3,000	£4,000	£5,000

6. The price of a barrel of oil in 1998, 1999 and 2000 rose 10% more over the previous year's price. How much more did the consumer have to pay in 2000 than in 1998?

A	B	C
19%	21%	23 %

7. Assume British Airways owns 40% of the stock in Virgin Atlantic Company. EasyJet owns 20,000 shares in Virgin. Midland owns all the shares not owned by British Airways or easyJet. How many shares does British Airways own if Midland has 25% more shares than British Airways?

A	B	C
80,000	75,000	100,000

8. A market research survey in England of *n* young people under 15 years found that 30% liked McDonald's. An additional *x* young people were asked and all of them liked McDonald's. Eighty per cent of all the young people in the market research survey claimed they liked McDonald's. Find *n* young people in terms of *x*.

A	B	C
3.5	2.5*n*	3

9. Peter, David and Tina ate lunch together. Tina's bill was 70% more than David's bill. Peter's bill was 11/9 as much as Tina's bill. If David paid £10 for his lunch, approximately how much was the total bill that the three paid?

A	B	C
£48	£52	£45

10. A surveyor assessed the value of a house in the North of England at £85,000. The assessed value represented only 50% of the market value of the house. If the Inland Revenue taxes are £5 for every £1,000 of the market value of the house, how much are the total taxes on the house?

A	B	C
£800	£637.5	£850

11. A ton of potatoes costs £20, a ton of onions cost £29. If the price of potatoes rises by 15% a month and the price of onions remains unchanged, how many months will it take before a ton of onions costs less than a ton of potatoes?

A	B	C
4	2	3

12. At one of the Save the Children Fund's charity banquets for wealthy people, 30% of the guests contributed £60 each, 55% contributed £15 each and the rest contributed £5 each. Approximately what percentage of the total banquet takings came from people who gave £15?

A	B	C
31%	42%	26%

13. A microwave oven originally cost £200. Before Christmas the microwave was on sale at 110% of its original cost. After the new year when the sale season started, the microwave was discounted 15% and was sold. The microwave was sold for what cost?

A	B	C
£253	£187	£220

14. There are 20 postmen in Crawley responsible for delivering mail. If a typical postman can deliver 30/2 mail in 30 minutes, how many mails should all postmen in Crawley be able to deliver in 3½ hours

A	B	C
2100	1050	2200

15. Butter costs ½ as much as cheese. Cheese costs 9/8 as much as milk. Milk costs what fraction of the cost of butter?

A	B	C
9/8	9/16	16/9

16. The total cost of typing a PhD thesis is £50. Merry typed 60% of the thesis and Lina typed the rest. How much did Lina receive?

A	B	C
£20	£25	£30

17. On Monday a milkman delivered *x* bottles of milk, on Tuesday he delivered 3 times as many, and on Wednesday he delivered 120 bottles. Over the 3 days the milkman delivered 240 bottles. How many did he deliver on Tuesday?

A	B	C
30	90	120

18. An estate agent rented a house for £500 per month. Ten years later the tenant calculated that if he had bought the house and had a £200 per month mortgage he would have owned the house. How much would he have saved if he had bought the house?

A	B	C
£30,000	£24,000	£36,000

19. A team exploring the Amazon consists of 30 scientists, of whom 1/3 are women, 2/3 are men. To obtain a team with 40% women, how many men should be replaced by women?

A	B	C
2	5	8

20. An ice cream machine produces 6,000 lollies per hour. Because of maintenance the ice cream machine is not operational for 22 minutes. How many lollies are not produced because of maintenance?

A	B	C
2225	2200	2275

21. The following are car production figures for plant A in a week: on Mon. 200 cars, on Tues. 300 cars, on Wed. 400 cars, on Thurs. 650 cars, on Fri. 210 cars. What was the average car production for the week for plant A?

A	B	C
350	300	352

Interpretation of graphs and data

To be able to calculate and measure statistical information is very important for jobs in IT, finance and management.

Tips

- Scan the whole graph or table before you start answering the questions.
- Carefully read the units, ie cm, m, pounds, pence, etc and make sure to answer in the correct unit.
- As before, read the choices before you answer, because many questions need a little calculation and more intelligent reading to understand them.
- A common mistake is mixing between decimals and percentages as shown in the example below:

  1/100 = 1% = 0.01
  10/100 = 10% = 0.1

- Always use your common sense to see if the answer makes sense.

Now work through the examples below and see how many you can finish in 25 minutes.

Figure 5.1 Continuous growth of sales and staff

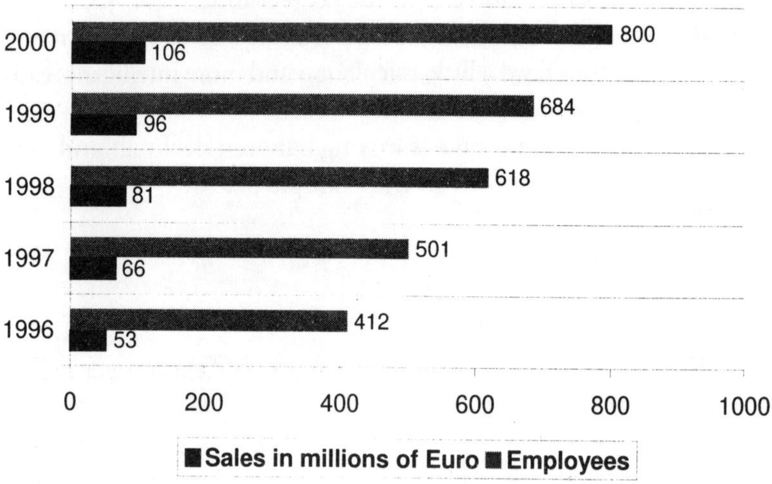

1. By approximately what percentage did total staff numbers change from year 1996 to 2000?

A	B	C
387	94%	90%

2. By what percentage did the total profit change from year 1996 to 2000?

A	B	C
100%	53 million EUR	50%

3. If the number of employees in the year 2001 has increased by 25% over 2000, what was the total number of new recruits in 2001 compared with 2000?

A	B	C
200	1000	1200

4. Between 1996 and 2000, which year showed the smallest and largest staff profit numbers?

A	B	C
1996 & 2000	1999 & 1996	1999 & 1998

5. If 1 euro = £0.65, then the profit in 1999 was approximately

A	B	C
£6,240,000	£62.4 million	€624,000,000

6. If there are 300 additional recruits in 2001 and the average growth of sales and staff remain constant, how much greater would the total sales volume in EUR for 2001 be?

A	B	C
£39.75 million	EUR 3,975,000	EUR 39,750,000

Figure 5.2 One week's temperatures in 3 Capitals

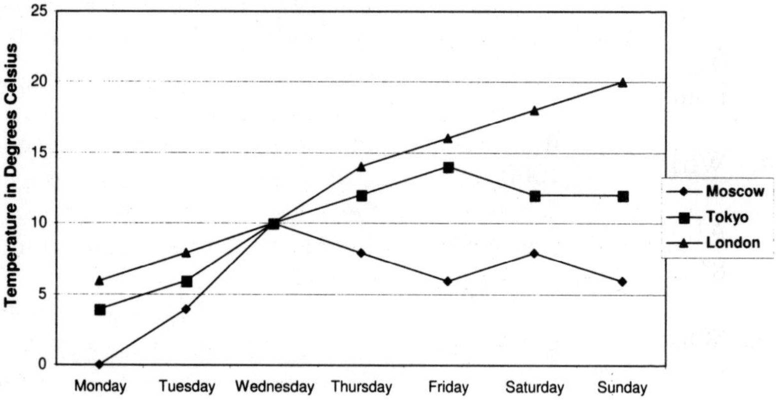

1. On which day did the three capitals have the same temperature?

A	B	C
Monday	Wednesday	Friday

2. Which day showed the largest increase in temperature in Moscow?

A	B	C
Wednesday	Saturday	Monday

3. In which capital was the trend of temperature consistent throughout the week?

A	B	C
London	Moscow	Tokyo

4. What was the average temperature for the week in Moscow?

A	B	C
8°	5.5°	6°

5. What was the average temperature for the week in Tokyo?

A	B	C
7°	8°	10°

6. What was approximately the percentage increase in temperature between Monday and Sunday in London?

A	B	C
237	233%	245

7. What was the ratio of temperature in London on Sunday to the temperature in Moscow on Tuesday?

A	B	C
5:1	1:5	4/20

Figure 5.3 Income and expenditure for average family between 1990 and 2000

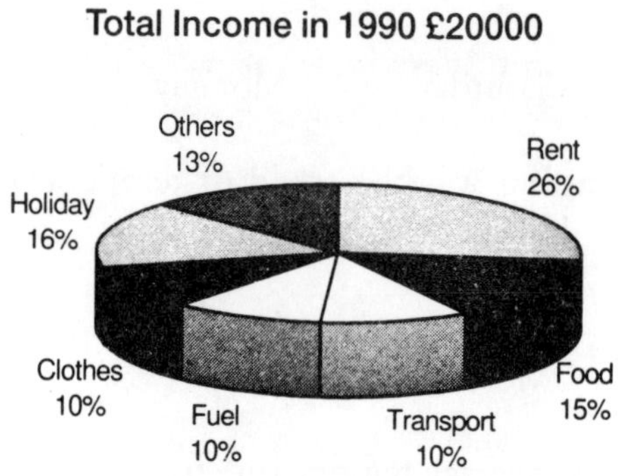

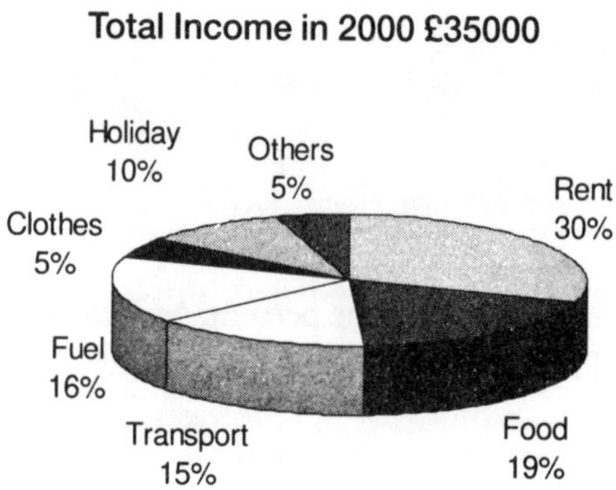

1. The yearly expenditure on holiday in 1990 was 160% of the amount spent on:

   A Transport in 1990
   B Food in 1990
   C Clothes in 2000

2. If the average family income in 2001 rises by 25% over 2000 (and all expenditure percentages remain the same), how much will the average family spend on holiday in 2001?

   A £3,650
   B £3,500
   C £4,375

3. The combined expenditure in 1990 for transport, fuel and others was approximately the same as

   A 2/3 the amount spent on rent in 1990
   B The amount spent on food in 2000
   C The amount spent on clothes and others in 2000

4. The combined average family expenditure in 2000 for fuel, food, clothes and holiday was what fraction of the annual income?

   A 2/3
   B ½
   C ¼

5. The amount spent on fuel in 2000 was the same as

   A The amount spent on transport in 1990
   B The amount spent on holiday in 1990
   C The combined amount spent on food and others in 1990

Figure 5.4 Number of cars sold in Europe

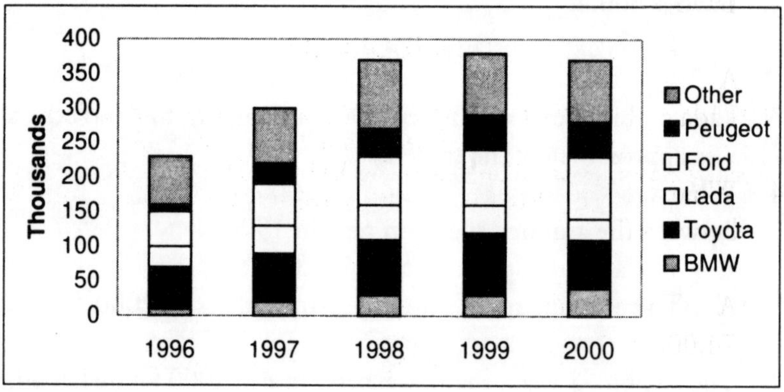

1. Approximately what percentage of cars sold in 2000 were Ford?

A	B	C
24%	30%	29%

2. From 1996 to 2000, of all the cars sold in Europe, the largest number of cars belonged to which manufacturer?

A	B	C
Ford	Peugeot	Toyota

3. Sales of which car showed the most consistent increase between 1996 and 2000?

A	B	C
Lada	Ford	Peugeot

4. What was the average yearly number of cars sold by Toyota between 1996 and 2000?

A	B	C
74,000	7 million	820,000

5. Between 1996 and 2000, Peugeot car sales increased by what percentage?

A	B	C
50%	400%	40%

6. Which year showed the largest increase in other car sales over total car sales between 1996 and 2000?

A	B	C
2000	1999	1998

Table 5.2 Numbers of undergraduates, postgraduates and graduates of five universities between 1998 and 2000

University	1998 in thousands			1999 in thousands			2000 in thousands		
	Undergraduates	Postgraduates	Graduates	Undergraduates	Postgraduates	Graduates	Undergraduates	Postgraduates	Graduates
AAA	10	2	2	12	1.5	2.5	13	1	3
BBB	15	4	3	14	3	3	12	2	2.5
CCC	20	4	5	22	4.1	5.2	23	4.2	5.5
DDD	18	2	2.5	19	1.5	3	21	1	3.1
EEE	22	1	4	23	0.5	4.1	25	0.5	4.2

1. Which university has shown a decline in undergraduate numbers every year over the period 1998–2000?

A	B	C
AAA	BBB	EEE

2. What was the percentage increase in the total undergraduate numbers in all five universities in 2000 as compared with 1998 (to the nearest 4%)?

A	B	C
7%	9	11%

3. Which universities had the same number of postgraduates and graduates between 1998 and 2000?

A	B	C
AAA	BBB	CCC
&	&	&
BBB	DDD	EEE

4. If in 2001 the number of undergraduate and postgraduate students in university EEE increased by 25% and 200% respectively over the year 2000, and the number of graduates remained the same, what approximately was the total number of undergraduates, postgraduates and graduates in university EEE in 2001?

A	B	C
369,500	0.3695 million	36,950

Table 5.3 Sales volume in five mobile phone companies over the last five years in thousands

Company	1996	1997	1998	1999	2000
Nokia	580	679	887	998	1187
Ericsson	294	493	548	598	632
Orange	192	232	268	312	366
Cellnet	120	209	204	302	366
BT	403	399	562	593	821

1. Which mobile phone companies have shown a decline in sales over the period 1996–2000?

A	B	C
Cellnet & BT	BT & Nokia	Ericsson & Cellnet

2. Of all these mobile phone companies, which showed a proportional increase in sales between 1999 and 2000, and which showed the smallest and the largest increase as compared to 1999?

A	B	C
Cellnet & Ericsson	Ericsson & BT	BT & Orange

3. For all companies combined, what is the percentage increase in sales between 1999 and 1998 (to the nearest 4%)?

A	B	C
11%	14%	12%

4. What is the average sales for Ericsson from 1996 to 2000?

A	B	C
0.05135 million	513,000	512,000

5. Which mobile company's sales volume in 2000 was approximately three times its sales in 1996?

A	B	C
Ericsson	Nokia	Cellnet

6. Which mobile company had the lowest increase in sales volume in 2000 as compared with 1997?

A	B	C
Orange	Ericsson	Nokia

Table 5.4 EU members' statistical information in 2000

Country	Population in millions	Total employment in millions	% under the poverty line	% unemployed women to the total unemployment	Total employment: unemployment
Portugal	10	5	29	49.5	2:1
Greece	12	6	24	57.5	5:2
UK	58	20	16	35.1	10:2
Spain	38	19	19	60.8	3:2
Italy	48	20	18	52.2	12:3
France	60	25	16	54.7	10:3
Netherlands	11	5.5	14	47.7	4:2
Belgium	13	5	13	30.5	8:3
Germany	68	34	13	58.5	9:3

1. Which country had the highest number of people under the poverty line in 2000?

A	B	C
France	UK	Spain

2. What was the total number of unemployed men in Italy in 2000, in millions?

A	B	C
2.29	2.39	2.61

3. The total number of unemployed women in 2000 was about *x* million in Belgium, with *x* equal to about

A	B	C
2.43	0.57	1.3

4. If in 2000 the unemployed women aged 60 or over made up only 1/3 of the total unemployed women in Greece, how many men aged 60 or over were unemployed?

A	B	C
Can't say	1.38 million	0.46 million

5. The ratio of population between France and Portugal in 2000 was?

A	B	C
10/60	1:6	6:1

6. Which countries had the highest and lowest number of unemployed men in 2000?

A	B	C
Spain & Greece	Germany & Portugal	Germany & Greece

In England and Wales, if you want to obtain a driving licence, first you should sit and pass your theoretical driving test. Then and only then can you apply to take a practical driving test. Table 5.5 shows the results of six practical driving test centres in England and Wales for all applicants in hundreds who passed and failed their driving test, assuming that the applicants took the theoretical and the practical test in the same year.

Table 5.5 The results of six driving test centres in England and Wales

Driving test centre	Result	1998	1999	2000	2001	2002
1. London	Passed	112	69	62	86	119
	Failed	121	96	102	89	191
2. Manchester	Passed	100	89	94	54	66
	Failed	116	99	96	58	68
3. Warwick	Passed	54	69	96	86	109
	Failed	95	130	97	84	112
4. Oxford	Passed	22	66	23	99	101
	Failed	44	87	44	102	111
5. Swansea	Passed	53	56	61	80	45
	Failed	62	75	72	81	50
6. Hull	Passed	70	82	70	31	10
	Failed	75	86	73	81	20

1. What was the total number of applicants in hundreds who passed the theoretical driving tests in 2001 and 2002?

A	B	C
931	1933	2159

2. In which year did more applicants pass their practical driving test than failed in Warwick?

A	B	C
1999	2000	2001

3. Of the total number who obtained a driving licence in 2002, what percentage was from Swansea?

A	B	C
10%	12.5%	15%

4. In which driving centre has the number of failed practical driving tests declined every year over the period 1998–2001?

A	B	C
Hull	London	Manchester

5. What was the ratio of the number of applicants who obtained a driving licence in Manchester in 1998 to the number who failed the practical driving test in Hull in 2002?

A	B	C
1:5	5:1	10:1

6. In which driving test centre did more applicants obtain a driving licence between 1999 and 2002?

A	B	C
Warwick	Can't say	London

Answers to practice exercises

Numerical estimation

1. B
2. A
3. C
4. D
5. B
6. C
7. D
8. A
9. B
10. C
11. B
12. A
13. D
14. B
15. A
16. D
17. B
18. C
19. A
20. B
21. D
22. C
23. A
24. D
25. C
26. C
27. A
28. B
29. D
30. B

Problem solving

1. A
2. B
3. C
4. B
5. C
6. B
7. A
8. B
9. A
10. C
11. C
12. A
13. B
14. A
15. C
16. A
17. B
18. C
19. A
20. B
21. C

Interpretation of graphs and data

Figure 5.1 Continuous growth of sales volume and staff

1. B
2. A
3. A
4. B
5. B
6. C

Figure 5.2 One week's temperature in three capitals

1. B
2. A
3. A
4. C
5. C
6. B
7. A

Figure 5.3 Income and expenditure for average family between 1990 and 2000

1. A
2. C
3. B
4. B
5. C

Figure 5.4 Number of cars sold in Europe

1. A
2. C

3. B
4. A
5. B
6. C

Table 5.2 Numbers of undergraduates, postgraduates and graduates of five universities between 1998 and 2000

1. B
2. C
3. A
4. C

Table 5.3 Sales volume in five mobile phone companies over the last five years, in thousands

1. A
2. B
3. B
4. B
5. C
6. A

Table 5.4 EU members' statistical information in 2000

1. A
2. B
3. B
4. A
5. C
6. A

Table 5.5 The results of six driving test centres in England and Wales

1. B
2. C
3. A
4. C
5. B
6. A

Tips on solving the problems in problem solving

1. The perimeter of the house is
   $25 + 25 + 75 + 75 = 200$
   The total cost = £10 × 200/0.5 = £4000, therefore A is correct.
2. The first 1000 books cost n pounds for each book, so altogether they will cost $1000n$. The total cost is
   $1000n + 6000 \times n/6 = 2000n$, therefore B is correct.
3. Distance = Speed × Time
   300 = 120 × Time; Time = 2.5 hours from London to Hull
   Total journey took 4 hours and 30 minutes, so the time from Hull to London is 4.5 – 2.5 = 2 hours
   Speed = 300/2 = 150 mph, therefore C is correct.
4. For 1 person it cost = $n + 1/9 \times 4n = 13/9n$. For 2 persons, multiply by two, therefore B is correct.
5. John sold his stock at = 2/3 × £3,000 = £2,000
   Value was doubled = 2 × £2,000 = £4,000; and he made a profit of
   £4,000 – £2,000 = £2,000
   The remaining stocks, £3,000 – £2,000 = £1,000, were sold at £1,000 × 4 = £4,000 and the profit he made was £4,000 – £1,000 = £3,000, therefore the total profit was £2,000 + £3,000 = £5,000, and therefore C is the correct answer.
6. Let X denote the price in 1998. In 1999 the price rose to 110% of X which is $(1.1)X$, and in 2000 the price rose to 110% of $(1.1)X$ which is $(1.1)(1.1)X$ or $1.21X$. Therefore the price of oil rose by 21% more in 2000.
7. If Midland owns 25% more than British Airways and British Airways owns 40% of Virgin Atlantic, then Midland must own 1.25 × 0.4 = 50% of Virgin Atlantic, since easyJet = 100% – 40% – 50% = 10%
   If 10% of the shares in Virgin Atlantic is 20,000 shares, then there must be 200,000 shares in Virgin Atlantic. British Airways'

shares are = 200,000 × 0.4 = 80,000, so that A is the correct answer.

8. The total number of people researched is
   $0.3n + x = 0.8\ (n + x)$
   $x = 2.5n$, so that B is the correct answer.
9. Tina = 1.7 David and Peter = 11/9 Tina, so Peter = 11/9 × 1.7 David = 2 David.
   David paid £10 for his lunch, therefore Peter paid £20 and Tina paid £17, and the total bill for the three of them was approximately £48.
10. First find the market value of the house, which means £85,000/ .5= £170,000. The tax rate is £5 for every £1,000 or 0.005. Therefore the total tax is 0.005 × £170,000 = £850.
11. The price of potatoes will be £20 $(1.15)^n$. After n months the price must be greater than £29/£20 = 1.45. Since 1.15 × 1.15 = 1.32 and 1.15 × 1.15 × 1.15 = 1.52, after three months the cost of a ton of onions will be less than the cost of a ton of potatoes.
12. Assume 100 people were invited. Therefore 30% represents 30, who contributed £60, and 55% represents 55 persons, who contributed £15, and the rest represents 15% or 15 persons who contributed £5. The total amount of contribution is £2,700, and the percentage of the total banquet takings coming from people who gave £15 = 825/£2,700 = 31%, therefore answer A is correct.
13. Since 110% of £200 = £220, before Christmas the microwave was offered for sale at £220. It was sold for (100% – 15%) = 85% of £220, since there was 15% discount. Therefore the microwave was sold for 0.85 × £220 = £187.
14. 30 minutes is ½ of an hour. Therefore in 3.5 hours the postmen should mail: 20 × 7 × 30/2 = 2,100 items of mail.
15. Butter = ½ Cheese, and Cheese = 9/8 Milk. Therefore Butter = ½ × 9/8 Milk, and Milk's cost as a fraction of Butter is Milk/ Butter = 16/9.

16. Merry typed 60% × £50 = 30, therefore Lina typed £20 worth of the PhD thesis.
17. Assume that on Monday the milkman delivered X bottles of milk, on Tuesday he delivered $3X$ and on Wednesday he delivered 120. The total is
    $X + 3X + 120 = 240$, therefore $X = 30$, and on Tuesday he delivered $3X = 3 \times 30 = 90$ bottles of milk.
18. Rent on the house for 10 years is £500 × 10 ×12 = £60,000. And if the tenant had bought the house the mortgage would have been £200 × 10 × 12 = £24,000. Therefore he would have saved £36,000.
19. We have 10 women and 20 men in the team. To obtain 40% women, 40%×30 = 12; we already have 10, so we need another 2. The answer is A.
20. Number of lollies per minute = 6000/60 = 100. We have 22 minutes × 100 = 2200.
21. The average = (200 + 300 + 400 + 650 + 210)/5 = 352.

Tips on solving the problems in interpretation of graphs and data

Figure 5.1 Continuous growth of sales and staff

1. In 1996 the total staff number was 412 and in 2000 the total staff number was 800. Therefore the total staff increase expressed as a percentage between 1996 and 2000 is
   (800 – 412)/412 × 100 = 94.17% »94%.
2. The total profit changes expressed as percentage between1996 and 2000 is
   (106 – 53)/53 × 100 = 100%.
3. Number of employees in the year 2001 is
   25% × 800 + 800 = 1000, and the total number of new recruits in 2001 is
   1000 – 800 = 200.
4. The staff profit ratio for 1996: 412/53 = 7.77
   1997: 501/66 = 7.59
   1998: 618/81 = 7.62
   1999: 684/96 = 7.125
   2000: 800/106 = 7.54
   Therefore in 1999 the staff profit ratio was the smallest, and in 1996 the largest.
5. If one euro is equivalent to £0.65, then profit in 1999 is
   96 × 0.65 = £62.4 million.
6. Total number of employees in 2001: 800 + 300 = 1,100, since the average growth of sales and staff remains constant compared to 2000. Therefore the total sales is
   (106 × 1100)/800 = 145.75 and this amount was greater than in 2000 by
   145.75 – 106 = 39.75 million euros = 39,750,000 euros. Check the decimal number in multiple choices carefully to ensure that the number is in million euros.

Figure 5.2 One week's temperatures in three capitals

1. The answer is B, since all three capitals have the same temperature.
2. The answer is A; the line shows the largest increase in temperature for a week in Moscow.
3. Scanning the graph, it is clear that London shows a consistent increase in temperature from Monday to Sunday.
4. The average temperature for the week in Moscow is $(0 + 4° + 10° + 8° + 6° + 8° + 6°)/7 = 6°$.
5. The average temperature for the week in Tokyo is $(4° + 6° + 10° + 12° + 14° + 12° + 12°)/7 = 10°$.
6. The temperature in London on Monday was 6° and on Sunday 20°, the approximate percentage increase over a week is $20° – 6°/6° \times 100 = 233.33\%$ » 233 %.
7. The temperature in London on Sunday was 20° and the temperature in Moscow on Tuesday was 4° so the ratio is $20°/4° = 5/1 = 5:1$.

Figure 5.3 Income and expenditure for average family between 1990 and 2000

1. Here you will find the ratio of the percentages. In 1990, 16% of the expenditure was for holidays. We want x where 160% of x – 16%, so x = 10%. Any category that received 10% of 1990 expenditures gives the correct answer. Simply by looking at the pie graph it is obvious that transport in 1990 is the correct answer.
2. The average family income in 2001: $25\% \times 35{,}000 + 35{,}000 = £43{,}750$

   If the percentage expenditure on holiday in 2001 is similar to 2000 and equals 10%, then the average family holiday expenditure on holiday in 2001: $£43{,}750 \times 10\% = £4375$.

3. By adding the percentages: transport, fuel and others in 1990 we get
   10% + 10% + 13% = 33%, therefore the combined expenditure is 33% × £20,000 = £6,600. Now you have to compare this figure with the three relationships given as multiple choices in A: 2/3 × 26% × £20,000 = £3466.66 which is not correct. Then B: 19% × £35,000 = £6,650. Finally C: 10% × £35,000 = £3,500 which is incorrect. Therefore B is the closest value and is the correct answer.
4. By adding all the expenditures: fuel, food, clothes and holiday we get 16% + 19% + 5% + 10% = 50% = 1/2, therefore B is the correct answer.
5. The amount spent on fuel in 2000 is 16% × 35,000 = £5,600. Now evaluate the three multiple choices to find any equivalent
   A: 10% × 20,000 = £2,000
   B: 16% × 20,000 = £3,200
   C: 15% + 13% = 28% × 20,000 =£5,600 which is the correct answer.

Figure 5.4 Number of cars sold in Europe

Comparing several categories using a graph of the cumulative type, where the bar is divided up proportionately among different quantities, needs careful evaluation of each quantity. To make the quantities clear to you and help you to understand the graph, I have prepared below a simple table with all quantities:

Year	BMW	Toyota	Lada	Ford	Peugeot	Other
1996	10	60	30	50	10	70
1997	20	70	40	60	30	80
1998	30	80	50	70	40	100
1999	30	90	40	80	50	90
2000	40	70	30	90	50	90

1. Total cars sold in 2000 in thousands were
40 + 70 + 30 + 90 + 50 + 90 = 370 and the percentage of Ford cars sold in 2000 is
90/370 × 100 = 24.32% » 24%.
2. To find which manufacturer sold the most cars simply calculate the numbers of cars sold in thousands between 1996 and 2000 for the three models given in your multiple choices:
Ford: 50 + 60 + 70 + 80 + 90 = 350
Peugeot: 10 + 30 + 40 + 50 + 50 = 180
Toyota: 60 + 70 + 80 + 90 + 70 = 370
Therefore the largest number of cars sold in thousands between 1996 and 2000 was by Toyota.
3. By scanning all the quantities in the table above, it is clear that Ford had consistently increased its car sales between 1996 and 2000.
4. The average number of cars sold by Toyota between 1996 and 2000 in thousands:
(60 + 70 + 80 + 90 + 70)/5 = 74. Make sure you know where the decimal point is and that the number is multiplied by thousands.
5. Peugeot car sales expressed as a percentage between 1996 and 2000 in thousands:
(50 – 10)/10 × 100 = 400%.
6. Scanning the table above, you find that in 1998 other car sales were the largest between 1996 and 2000.

Table 5.2 Numbers of undergraduates, postgraduates and graduates of five universities between 1998 and 2000

1. Simply scanning the table may be the best strategy here. All you need to do is find only one of the three universities given in the multiple choices where the number of undergraduates

declined between 1998 and 2000. Here University BBB shows a decline in undergraduate numbers every year over the period 1998–2000 and is the correct answer.

2. *Important note.* Carefully add all the figures in questions like this, otherwise the round number may be calculated differently and that may lead you to choose the wrong answer in multiple choices, which are deliberately designed with the options very near to each other.

   Total undergraduate number in thousands in all five universities in 1998 was

   10 + 15 + 20 + 18 + 22 = 85

   Total undergraduate number in thousands in all five universities in 2000 was

   13 + 12 + 23 + 21 + 25 = 94

   The increase expressed as a percentage: (94 – 85)/85 × 100 = 10.58% = 11%.

3. Scanning the table carefully for all five universities, you will find that university AAA has 2,000 postgraduates and graduates in 1998 and university BBB has 3,000 postgraduates and graduates in 1999. No other university shows similar characteristics. Therefore AAA & BBB is the correct answer.

4. In 2001 the number of undergraduates in thousands in university EEE:

   25% × 25 + 25 = 31,250

   The number of postgraduates in 2001 is 200% × 0.5 + 0.5 = 1500 respectively. However, the number of graduates remains the same for 2001, then the total number is

   4200 + 31,250 + 1500 = 36,950. Again check your decimal point carefully.

Table 5.3 Sales volume in five mobile phone companies over the last five years in thousands

1. By scanning the table for all five mobile companies, you will find that Cellnet and BT have shown a decline in sales over the period 1996–2000.
2. All five mobile companies showed an increase in sales between 1999 and 2000
   Nokia's increase was: 1187 – 998 = 189, therefore the proportional increase was 189/998 = 0.189
   Ericsson's increase was: 632 – 598 = 34, therefore the proportional increase was 34/598 = 0.056
   Orange's increase was: 366 – 312 = 54, therefore the proportional increase was 54/312 = 0.173
   Cellnet's increase was: 366 – 302 = 64, therefore the proportional increase was 64/302 = 0.211
   BT's increase was: 821 – 593 = 228, therefore the proportional increase was 228/593 = 0.384
   Therefore the smallest proportional increase is 0.056 (for Ericsson) and the largest proportional increase is 0.384 (for BT).
3. The total sales in thousands for all mobile companies in 1998:
   887 + 548 + 268 + 204 + 562 = 2469
   and in 1999:
   998 + 598 + 312 + 302 + 593 = 2803
   The increase expressed as a percentage: (2803 – 2469)/2469 × 100 = 13.52 % and to the nearest 4% is 14%.
4. The average sales for Ericsson in thousands between 1996 and 2000 is
   (294 + 493 + 548 + 598 + 632)/5 = 513,000.
5. Scan the table for all five mobile companies and you will find that Cellnet's sales were 366,000 in 2000 compared to 120,000 in 1996, which is approximately three times and is the correct answer.

6. Scan the table for the three multiple choices: Orange, Ericsson, Nokia, and don't waste time by calculating others not included. The lowest increase in sales in thousands for Orange between 1997 and 2000 was 366 – 232 = 134 and for Ericsson 632 – 493 = 139 and for Nokia 1187 – 679 = 508. Therefore Orange has the lowest increase in sales volume in 2000 as compared with 1997.

Table 5.4 EU members' statistical information in 2000

1. Again, only perform the calculation for the three countries given in your multiple choices and don't waste time.
   Number of people in millions under the poverty line in France:
   16% × 60 = 9.6
   Number of people in millions under the poverty line in the UK:
   16% × 58 = 9.28
   Number of people in millions under the poverty line in Spain:
   19% × 38 = 7.22
   Therefore France has the highest number and A is correct.
2. Let x be the total unemployment (men and women), then for Italy
   Total employment/Total unemployment in millions: $12/3 = 20/x$
   $x = 5$ million unemployed (men and women), from which 52.2% × 5 = 2.61 million are unemployed women and 5 – 2.61 = 2.39 million are unemployed men.
3. Let x be the total unemployment (men and women), then for Belgium
   Total employment/Total unemployment in millions in Belgium: $8/3 = 5/x$
   x= 1.875 million unemployed (men and women), from which 1.875 × 30.5% = 0.57 million are unemployed women.

4. We Can't say, because there is no information in the table which shows any details of unemployed men or women aged 60 or over. The table has only general unemployment figures; therefore, we cannot answer the question.
5. The ratio of population between France and Portugal in millions: 60/10 = 6/1 = 6:1.
6. Total employment/Total unemployment in millions in Spain:
   $3/2 = 19/x$; $x = 12.66$
   60.8% × 12.66 = 7.697 million women and **4.9627** million men unemployed
   Total employment/Total unemployment in millions in Greece:
   $5/2 = 6/x$; $x = 2.4$
   57.5% × 2.4 = 1.38 million women and **1.02** million men unemployed
   Total employment/Total unemployment in millions in Germany: $9/3 = 34/x$; $x = 11.33$
   58.5% × 11.33 = 6.629 million women and **4.703** million men unemployed
   Total employment/Total unemployment in millions in Portugal:
   $2/1 = 5/x$; $x = 2.5$
   49.5% × 2.5 = 1.237 million women and **1.2625** million men unemployed

   It is clear that Spain has the highest and Greece the lowest number of unemployed men.

Table 5.5 The results of six driving test centres in England and Wales

1. The total number of applicants in hundreds who passed the theoretical driving test is equal to all the applicants who took the practical driving test, whether passed or failed
   In 2001: 86 + 89 + 54 + 58 + 86 + 84 + 99 + 102 + 80 + 81 + 31 + 81 = 931

In 2002: 119 + 191 + 66 + 68 + 109 + 112 + 101 + 111 + 45 + 50 + 10 + 20 = 1,002
Therefore the total number who passed the theoretical driving test in 2001 and 2002 is
931 + 1,002 = 1,933. B is the correct answer.

2. By scanning Table 5.5, you will find that only in 2001 in Warwick was the number of applicants who passed the driving test (86) higher than the number who failed the test (84). Therefore C is the correct answer.
3. The total number of applicants in hundreds who obtained a driving licence is
119 + 66 + 109 + 101 + 45 + 10 = 450
The percentage is 45/450 × 100 = 10%.
Therefore A is the correct answer.
4. By scanning the table carefully for the three choices given, you will find that only in Manchester has the number who failed the practical test dropped year on year: 116 (1998), 99 (1999), 96 (2000) and 58 (2001). Therefore C is the correct answer.
5. The number of applicants who obtained driving licences in Manchester in 1998 is 100 and the number who failed the practical driving test in Hull in 2002 is 20. Therefore the ratio is 100/20 = 5:1. Therefore B is the correct answer.
6. This can be answered by adding all who passed the driving test between 1999 and 2002 for the two chosen centres; the results in hundreds are
Warwick: 69 + 96 + 86 + 109 = 360; London: 69 + 62 + 86 +119 = 336
Warwick has the greatest number. Therefore A is the correct answer.